27 QUESTIONS TO MAKE YOU SWEAT

A Workout Guide for Your Soul

Gregg Sulzer
with Patrick McCord, PhD

Published by
Hybrid Global Publishing
301 E 57th Street, 4th fl
New York, NY 10022

Copyright © 2019 by Gregg W. Sulzer

All rights reserved. No part of this book may be reproduced or transmitted in any form or by in any means, electronic or mechanical, including photocopying, recording, or by any information storage and retrieval system, without the written permission of the Publisher, except where permitted by law.

Manufactured in the United States of America, or in the United Kingdom when distributed elsewhere.

Sulzer, Gregg
    27 Questions to Make You Sweat: A Workout Guide for Your Soul
    LCCN: 2019914580
    ISBN: 978-1-948181-76-1
    eBook: 978-1-948181-77-8

Cover design by: Rachel Griffin and Justin Negard
Cover photo by: Justin Negard
Interior design: Claudia Volkman

GWSCoaching.com

Disclaimer: All of the events in this book actually happened and the dialogue is accurate to the best of my memory. The names have been changed for the obvious reasons. However, my sister, Lizzie, and my brother, Scott, have graciously given permission to use their names.

TABLE OF CONTENTS

Preface by Patrick McCord v
Introduction 1
1. Do You Examine Your Life? 9
2. How Do You Create More Peace in Your Life?.....................19
3. What Makes You Angry? 27
4. How Do You Spend Your Time? 35
5. How Do Your Insecurities Hold You Back? 41
6. How Does It Feel When You Lie? 49
7. When Is Enough Money Enough?.....................................57
8. Do You Have a Consistent Moral Code? 69
9. Do You Have One Secret Fear That Is Your
Constant Companion? 75
10. How Do You Know What You Know? 83
11. How Does Your Perspective Aid or Hinder You? 101
12. How Much of Your Life Do You Hide? 107
13. Do You Ever Talk About Death? 113
14. How Do You Respond When Someone Argues
with You? 123
15. With Your Romantic Partner, When Do You
Express Attraction? 131
16. Do You Take Full Responsibility for All
Your Actions? 139
17. Have You and Your Partner Defined What You Both Want

in Terms of Romantic Commitment? 145
18. What Do You Know About the Buddha? 153
19. What Do You Know About Jesus? 165
20. How Often Are You Motivated by Guilt? 177
21. Are You an Addict? How Long Would You Stay
in a Relationship with an Addict? 187
22. How Important Is It to Police Language Use? 205
23. What Part Do You Play in Economic Justice? 217
24. Are You a Forgiving Person? 239
25. Have You Ever Inappropriately Forced Your Will on Someone? Have You Yourself Ever Been Coerced by Some Kind of Threat? 249
26. What Is Unconditional Love? 257
27. Who Is the Most Powerful Person on the Planet? 271
Afterword 285
My Heartfelt Plea 287
Acknowledgments 289

PREFACE

A few years ago, a writing student of mine urged me to take on an editorial project. A friend of his had written a book of "useful" questions. I asked what authority this writer had—was he a PhD who had made a startling discovery? Had he survived terrible catastrophes or fought in an unspeakable war? Was he famous for artistic innovations? Was he a genius who had escaped the notice of the world?

"Nope. He's just a guy. But he's really earned his ideas," came the response.

I wasn't sure how much time I would have for this new project. I'd just begun work with Pulitzer Prize reporter Bill Dedman on *Empty Mansions: The Mysterious Life of Huguette Clark and the Spending of a Great American Fortune*. In a year it would become a *New York Times* bestseller, but Dedman had just handed me a 200,000-word manuscript that needed to be cut in half, for starters, and then, where was the story amongst the facts? Coming down the pike on Dedman's recommendation was another 200,000-word manuscript to cut and reshape: Mark Fallon's explosive *Unjustifiable Means*. And in addition to my usual teaching load, I was working on my own research into cognitive paradigms for long-form fiction and screenplay revision.

This sweaty question thing was a long shot.

But I knew my student who recommended Gregg was very

smart and generally astute, so I agreed to meet with and then, after much consideration, eventually to work with this writer-guy, Gregg Sulzer. From the beginning, Gregg told me he wanted to write a book of challenges—a series of questions to inspire readers to think more deeply about their lives, and by thinking deeply, possibly enhance and deepen their lived experiences. As a result of that internal questioning, a reader might come to a better understanding of their beliefs, morals, and life goals, and in a best case, there might be an epiphany or two.

In writing, as in life, intentions matter. And Gregg's intentions were, to my way of thinking, more than just interesting—they were generous, complicated, and clearly meaning to enhance what a philosopher would call "the good life."

But we all know what kinds of bricks good intentions make if you're going to pave a road and where that road eventually leads. Writing an entire book is much harder than anyone outside of publishing thinks it is.

Gregg also was sure he'd sell loads of books.

So we had a couple problems.

Would-be writers who tell me their great idea will make them money before they've written it are almost always "all show and no go." They talk the talk, but they've got zero walk. I wanted to know if Gregg was up to doing the real work of book-writing. Also, I may sound fussy, but I only want to work with writers who believe in their work so much that they'll write the book just because they love writing it, not to make piles of cash.

But then Gregg came to me with a draft already done. Not just a first draft, but a much-revised draft. He was ready for me to correct his punctuation, and then, off to the printing presses.

OK, he loved the idea enough to write and revise an entire manuscript, but . . .

Preface

Um . . . no, Gregg. I was sad to say that, in my editorial opinion, if he was sincere about his intention about creating a provocative and well-argued passel of questions, he'd have to do more work. Starting with tossing much of his much-revised draft.

I don't need to tell you that he wasn't ecstatic about that opinion. Yet, amazingly, he did what I asked and began the process of rethinking his approach. He agreed to include stories from his life—the life of "a guy" whose experiences were, for the most part, like most people's.

There were a few exceptions, but really, Gregg was a poor man's Socrates. He asked provoking questions of other people. He studied various wisdom traditions. He meditated. He tried to elicit honesty from others, and he demanded it of himself. He'd tried to live a life based on that thing Socrates did: finding the truth behind the illusions of money, status, conventional morality, finger-popping hipness, and big business propaganda that we're surrounded by. And like Socrates, Gregg was energetic and determined and unafraid.

So we worked together for a couple of years and several drafts. Finally, Gregg got tired of simply being edited and demanded of me a more determined and exact effort. Last year, we began going over what he'd written sentence by sentence, word by word, revising the questions, changing the order and the title, rethinking some of the fundamental ideas—and this book is the end result of that labor. It hasn't been easy; it has undoubtedly been sweaty. In fact, in the course of writing the book, we've both test-driven the challenges that come after every question.

I will tell you that, in all honesty, I have been very uncomfortable with some of my findings. But I'm also certain that my life has substantially changed for the better as a result of the process.

27 QUESTIONS TO MAKE YOU SWEAT

Your mileage may—as they say—vary.

But I assure you that if you answer the questions at the end of every chapter, you won't escape making some interesting discoveries. It's possible that you may be a bit more grateful and loving as well; you might even break a bad habit or two. Who knows?

Like all books, *27 Questions to Make You Sweat* has a point of view. So to be clear, the questions all have a moral or ethical dimension. We touch on religion, government, addiction, self-control, cognitive psychology and other sciences, as well as social theory. Almost every question goes through four steps:

1. The question
2. An anecdote or short story from Gregg's life
3. A discussion, in which we define terms, marshal facts, or quote sources, sometimes offer logical arguments, and conclude with some insights
4. A "Sweat This Out" section in which you, the reader, are invited to grab a notebook and fifteen minutes of thinking time and jot down observations, make lists of ideas, find someone to talk to, or even reach back into your memory

The sweaty part of this book is a gym for your moral and ethical beliefs. You will have to dig down into your life, your past, and your beliefs and haul up your most emotional and formative experiences. Write fast. Take whatever comes up. If something doesn't seem right, come back and change it later. Try to give full, fast, and spontaneous responses. Don't be afraid to just get goofy or extreme. These are ideas for you to *play with*. It's not the SATs. You can't get these questions wrong; if your answer is true,

Preface

it's right! You will have to make discoveries and learn new things.

We suggest you get a spiral notebook and handwrite your notes rather than use a computer. There is a powerful cognitive benefit to handwriting—you think more deeply and more slowly—and you will have your notebook when you're done.

In a perfect world, you might agree to go through the book with a friend or even a group. The questions are designed so that different people will make different discoveries, have different opinions, relate from different perspectives. But if you do, we'd advise that you build an escape hatch into your process; first, so that if something troubling or embarrassing shows up, you won't feel obligated to overshare if you don't want to. Second, it may also be a good idea to have an agreement about only calm discussion. Shouting or anger is probably a sign of fear, and you should build in a work-around for that situation.

And lastly, a word of warning about doing this with your spouse or beloved: you will either get to a deeper love or fall out of love or find yourself agreeing to disagree. We hope for the former, but we know well that all intimate relationships involve certain unexplored realms. Twenty-seven questions can reveal a vast amount of undiscovered country . . .

Please test your beliefs with these questions. We imagine that we're creating a playground, not a battlefield, so don't get all serious and pouty because things aren't complicated enough; give simplicity a chance. Play around with *your thoughts, your habits, your feelings, and your own sense of what a "good life" looks like* as you engage with the terms of these questions. See what happens. Playing is the best way to learn and grow. More than anything, we hope that when you break a sweat, it's the sweat that comes from playing hard and enjoying the game.

This isn't philosophy in the way a college class would teach it—abstract ideas presented in difficult readings—but it's philosophy the way "a guy" has put it together, in his own way and in his own time. You will have to dig down into *your* past, *your* beliefs, and *your* life, and test them all for fear or love.

—Patrick McCord

INTRODUCTION

A book can change your life. When I was nineteen, the woman I was involved with—who wasn't really my girlfriend, although she performed some of the behaviors of a girlfriend; who wasn't really my friend, although she performed some of the behaviors of a friend; who wasn't really my mom, although she was almost old enough to be my mom—gave me a book when she was moving out of her 15,000-square-foot stone palace she had called home. Her TV series had been cancelled in LA, she'd finished divorcing her fifth husband, and it was time to move. She was throwing books into a big black garbage bag when she came across *Think on These Things* by J. Krishnamurti. She tossed it to me and said, "You should check this out." Not exactly a passionate plea or an excited endorsement, but I knew from the year and a half we'd been together that she had a certain knowledge about the world which I definitely didn't have. If she believed something could potentially help me, I was all for it.

I had moved away from my broken family home a year and a half earlier and was struggling with "the meaning of life"—or if that sounds too grandiose, the meaning of my life. Not unusual for a young person, fresh from the nest. Krishnamurti had one key insight that, to this day, is still a cornerstone of my belief system:

27 QUESTIONS TO MAKE YOU SWEAT

> You must have, not strength, but confidence—the tremendous confidence which comes when you know how to think things out for yourself. . . . It is the function of right education to help you to think for yourself, so that out of your own thinking you feel immense confidence. Then you are a creative human being and not a slavish machine.

That book got me on the path to "confident knowing." I wanted to educate myself to know how I got here, what I'm supposed to be doing here, and how I could create my life so that I would be healthy and happy.

I wrote this book for curious people who have the same questions I had. Old, young, middle-aged and Midwestern, bicoastal, cysgender and bisexual, unreconstructed Confederates and radical feminists, along with Inuit, immigrants, old money and the newly poor—this book is for all of you who want to think more deeply about your life, your happiness, your relationships.

I like to think of it as equal opportunity sweating. Why will you sweat? I've tried to pose questions that provoked me in my life, and then offer some of what I've discovered to challenge you into a confrontation with yourself. The idea is to help you see your beliefs about the world in a dynamic context of information and associations. The questions are just a game for you to play, an organized approach to difficult concepts that I hope you find both challenging and enlightening, but if you play this game, you're going to have to wrestle with yourself, and in that struggle, you should get a hell of a workout. In the end, you're going to get yourself into good moral, ethical, maybe even spiritual shape. The more effort, the more you sweat discovering your personal truths, the better the result. There is no grading system and no judgments. You can ponder one question for a year if you want.

Introduction

We all develop at different rates, but the most important thing is that we continue to develop.

I was born privileged. On the privileged meter, if one was "You have to do lots of things you don't wanna do," and ten was "You can do whatever you want," I started out as a solid nine. My dad was a successful psychoanalyst in Westchester County, New York, and he believed in giving his children the best of everything. In the summers we had a beach house in the Hamptons and in the winters a ski house in Vermont. We shopped at Bloomingdales, belonged to the country club, and had a food service come and pack our refrigerator and freezer once a month. We lived in a million-dollar home on a private lake designed by my parents. My brother, sister, and I played many sports from the time we were four years old. We took music lessons, went to Broadway shows, went to concerts at famous jazz clubs, and had lavish parties in our beautiful lake house.

At ten years old I settled on tennis as my life sport. I had started ice-skating at four, skiing at five, ice hockey at six, baseball at seven, and by twelve or thirteen, I had quit everything except tennis. I became obsessed. I was good, and I wanted to go pro. I wanted to be number one in the world.

But . . .

When I was sixteen, my dad lost his license to practice, because he was a lying, cheating sociopath. Within six months, the bank repossessed our home, we moved into a rental house with no phone, heat every few days, food now and again, and parents that fought all the time. My dad started driving a cab.

Meanwhile Bill, the owner of my tennis club, informed me that my dad hadn't paid any of my tennis bills for two years, so I owed my club and my coach lots of money. Bill felt bad for me, so when people called the club asking for a private coach at their house, he would recommend me. I was sixteen years old; I had never given a private lesson before. My first client was the guy Michael Douglas portrayed in the movie *Wall Street*, Gordon Gekko. Gordon Gekko was based on this guy I was teaching. That same year I started teaching another famous billionaire whose name is plastered on university buildings and cultural institutions around New York City.

Gekko and his wife warmed to me— I went to parties with their family, they lent me money to buy a car, they bought me gifts for Christmas. Then one day they just stopped calling. But by now the billionaire's family had warmed up to me; I stayed very warm and cozy with them until fifteen years later when I was brusquely thrown out of their circle of trust accused of blasphemy and betrayal.

By age eighteen my family life was completely chaotic. Even though I was still living at home, financially I was completely on my own. After my dad paid the rent, there was literally no money for anything. OK, that's a bit dramatic. He would go to the gas station and fill up a five-gallon jug of diesel fuel about three to four days a week, depending on how many passengers had been in his cab that week, and give us the choice of heat in the morning or heat at night. The other days without fuel we'd sleep in our parkas, hats, socks, and when it got really cold, our gloves.

I had started playing drums at age ten. I had never really entertained the idea of being a professional musician, but when my dad ran out of money and playing tennis became too expensive, I switched my focus to music. At least practicing and playing music was free.

So I'm eighteen years old and still in high school, but ostensibly I'm living like an adult. I paid all my own bills, I had a job, a car, a girlfriend, and basically no reason to listen to my

Introduction

parents. I mean, why? My dad paid the rent, but he also took most of my money while I was living there. He knew where I kept my money, and of course I moved it, but it didn't stop him from trying. When he couldn't find it, he would put on his brilliantly misguided therapist hat and use total manipulation and guilt-tripping to get my money.

I decided I needed to move out. So a few months before college, I asked the mom of one of my other tennis clients if she knew of any places for rent in the area. It just so happened that her very successful lawyer husband was owed a favor from one of his very famous movie star clients, who happened to own a guesthouse.

She was eighteen years my senior, and when I moved into her guesthouse, she was in LA shooting a TV show that, months later, was cancelled. In her mid-twenties, she starred in a film that mysteriously became one of those blockbuster films—the kind that transformed her into an international star seemingly overnight. After she flew back East, we had a very active love affair for the next year and a half. The first time we had sex, she looked at me with her insanely beautiful, confused, addicted greenish-blue eyes and said—with as much passion as she could muster after three hours in what could only be described as a love scene from some crazy psychedelic B-movie about a waning Hollywood starlet and her young stud tennis pro lover—"I love you." But there wasn't any real love going on between us. As much as she loved professing the most powerful four-letter word in the universe, I always knew she was just acting.

I like to believe I've learned some of the big lessons, such as don't lie, don't cheat, don't kill, tell the truth as much as possible, and treat all people equally. And treat all people equally means that you treat the dishwasher with the same respect and honor as you treat your mother.

27 QUESTIONS TO MAKE YOU SWEAT

Spending all that intimate quality time on the inside of that much power, fame, and money while living so much on the outside of that power, fame, and money has given me a rather unique perspective on what really matters.

My intention for this book is to ask a series of questions that have been useful to me, questions I hope will encourage you to look deeper into yourself and help you overcome your limitations, blind spots, childhood traumas, and less-than-healthy perceptions of yourself. Thinking about life, beliefs, and values has helped me heal my dysfunctional past and connect more deeply with other people, friends, lovers, family, and even casual acquaintances. I'm posing questions so you can play with the ideas in your own mind and come to your own conclusions on your path to peace and happiness.

I've read hundreds of books on the mind-body-soul connection; I've sat for years in meditation; I've done yoga every day for decades; I've had an experience with Christ; I've got my life coaching certification; I've argued with the billionaires over tea; I've spent decades in therapy; played drums with kids in Africa; and contemplated the universe in a Buddhist Temple in the Himalayas. But I'm really just a guy with a broken heart that wants to see people go through life with less pain.

This book is not meant to be a long argument, but rather short bursts of inquiry. You can think about a particular question, perhaps writing down your ideas while sitting at a bus stop, riding on a train, or waiting for a youngster at soccer practice. As you sweat out the questions, small changes may happen; by the end of the book, you may have a different set of tools and ideas to assist you in thinking about yourself, your morality, your community, and your goals.

I want to address the God question now because you will

Introduction

hear me use the word periodically throughout the book. I am not a practitioner of an established religion in any way, shape, or form, but I believe deeply in my connection to an energy/spirit/consciousness that I call God. I like to call my belief system "The New Good News": It's great if you believe in God because it's all about God. It's also great if you don't believe in God because it doesn't really matter if you believe in God or not to lead a happy, healthy, balanced life. And it's also great if you just believe in science because real scientists are interested in the truth, and anyone that sincerely believes in God is also after the truth. A symptom of truth is the absence of fear, or more simply, the presence of love. So when you see the word *God*, know that I'm signifying an energy of truth and love and you can make your own interpretation. Most definitely I'm not referring to an old guy with a long beard sitting in a giant chair judging us.

How we view the world's events and how we let those events affect us are up to us. Perception is a choice. We can choose to punish, or we can choose to forgive.

Peace in,
GWS

1. DO YOU EXAMINE YOUR LIFE?

Socrates claimed that "The unexamined life is not worth living." Our lives get value from our beliefs. Socrates was urging us to think about core beliefs—religion, family, job, friends, relationships, political party—and seriously consider changing something. When was the last time you admitted that you were wrong?

Sphere of Fear or Circle of Love

In the Sphere of Fear, people are certain. They know the right way to do things. They tell themselves they are moral islands in an ocean of immorality. They "tough out" uncomfortable situations or relationships, and the very notion of questioning authority is immoral.

The Circle of Love is filled with people who know that there's much they don't know. They're looking for truth, and the looking part is the fun part. When life is taxing, absurd, or frustrating, they're open to the idea that they don't have all the answers. They're willing to take the time to be curious about other possibilities.

I'd been on the phone with my sister for about half an hour when we started to slide down a familiar rabbit hole.

> "Lizzy, it's all about the inner dialogue. The outer world is just a reflection of what our mind is creating."
> "Why does everything have to be so deep with you? Jesus, you drive me crazy. We can't just have a simple conversation."
> "I'm sorry, Lizzy, you're right. What am I thinking, wasting your time by questioning your beliefs with facts? Who cares about stinkin' reality when you're so comfortable with the way you've decided to see the world? Admit it, you chose that belief about 'lazy people' because it makes you better than 'them.' Shouldn't a Catholic like you see your neighbor—who is struggling to survive—as a person you should 'love as yourself'?"
> "What does my religion have to do with it?"
> "'Love thy neighbor as thyself,' some guy said—what's his name? Oh right, Jesus. And you know he was a socialist, right? The loaves and fishes? That's all Catholic stuff you say you believe in, right?"
> "Puhleeeze, Gregg, it's like you want me to be confused by knowing all this shit. It's not my job. And anyway, Real Housewives has already started, so I gotta go now..."

This was a familiar conversation with Lizzie. Our belief systems are pretty far apart, and as a result, we fight. It's uncomfortable, and to some degree, fear-based. Neither one of us is willing to actively examine ourselves and our ideas, and then adjust our ideas to reach agreement, or at least not fight; instead, we use these conversations to prove to ourselves how right we are.

If, in Socrates' terms, I'm going to examine my life, and in particular, this habit of no-win fighting, I have to look at what's really happening. The pretense is a conversation that inevitably turns into a debate about the meaning of the welfare state or government spending or greed versus poverty in the richest

1. Do You Examine Your Life?

nation on earth. Since we have this kind of argument over and over, there's some way that we're both getting what we want, yet we pretend that we want to change each other's minds. If we keep reenacting similar conversations yet our minds never change, we're not really examining our ideas, but we are getting what we want.

What do we want? Unconsciously, we want to fight. It could be sibling rivalry, by which a brother and sister can misunderstand each other and both of us need to be right because we can't bear to admit our sibling has any advantage over us. Sometimes these conversations leave both of us feeling impatient and more than a little angry, symptoms that we're slipping into the Sphere of Fear.

Why would we want that? Our dad was psychologically dangerous to himself and his family, and we learned to be hyperaware of his moods, and then we had to deal with his shortcomings: anger, irrational demands, substance abuse. Our mom loved us, but she was not strong enough to protect us from Dad's dysfunction. Lizzie and I shared this volatile climate of fear, anger, and frustration; we shared it in a very intimate and formative way. If I examine our childhood experiences, one thing is certain—we were filled with fear. You'd think that would make us similar, wouldn't you?

We love each other, and that's why we continue to keep in touch with each other. But when we dig a little deeper regarding our lived experiences, our core beliefs don't really offer any common ground to agree on. Arguments are inevitable.

And here's the kicker—when we argue, we feel the exciting intimacy of behaving like the children we were. Intimacy that we can't feel with any other human beings. Intimacy that united us when our father was at his worst. Except now we're adults, and there's no looming threat. This is a case where, although we've become such different people, the dysfunctional fighting comforts us because it's something we can share. And yet what we're sharing is a variety of fear. Ironically, if we didn't fight, we might not have much to say to one another . . .

So this is a classic example of Socrates insisting that I should examine what's going on. I have to decide if I—Mr. Love—am going to be cool with fighting as intimacy. I come away from those conversations with feelings of frustration, anger, impatience with my sister's shortsightedness—and I'm pretty sure she's feeling the same way about me. We both want intimacy, but on some level, we don't know how to have *loving* intimacy. Instead we relive our shared fears. For Lizzy and me, our fearful intimacy recreates our habits of "safe" emotion when we were children living in a dysfunctional household. This ritual behavior is what our father, the psychoanalyst, would call a classic case of "arrested development."

Dammit. I hate it when he's right.

Arrested development is when adults revert to childish behavior despite having tools to better negotiate their relationships. It's not a good thing. Getting out of this cycle requires that we grow up in some way. We need to have a new conversation—we need to examine together fresh ideas that will lead to a clearer consciousness of what we're doing. This is where examination helps.

Even as I'm writing this, I'm wondering if we can even do this. As a first step, we need to find the agreements. (The habits of disagreement are very powerful.) I might have to start out by saying, "I want to find a way to have conversations with you that lead to agreements on important issues, so we avoid those crappy dysfunctional feelings we're both still dragging around from childhood." I will have to give up proving that my beliefs

1. Do You Examine Your Life?

are right and instead enlist Lizzie to see if there is any overlap in our belief systems. Can we agree to find ways of expressing gratitude, admiration, and respect, which are all emotions that tell us we're in the Circle of Love?

I know this isn't going to be easy . . . but this is where I feel Socrates' sandal hitting my butt: Bam! "Yo. The very act of examination means struggle: if there are people or circumstances in your life that are uncomfortable, frustrating, confusing, those are areas that beg for examination. That's what I'm talkin' about."

If you and I are willing to *notice* those frustrations, then the struggle is already in process. You are already feeling the invisible, habitual confines of an idea box that is in some way jailing you. If you want to get outside that box and find a better way of doing things, you'll have to go deeper into the process of examination.

As I look toward reaching a more loving basis with Lizzie, I can predict that this examination will demand three things from me that are always in short supply: time, energy, and contemplation.

For all of us, taking the time, making the effort, and focusing in a contemplative way is difficult. It's almost as if we have to slow down the habitual motors that every aspect of our life is based on and put our efforts on the parts of life we *can't normally see*. After all, "outside the box" is outside the box we live in; it's outside the realm of our habits. Most of us get zero training in noticing habits or trying out unfamiliar ideas. Schools, no matter what their funding or information basis, are all too often nothing more than assembly lines making us into mild, agreeable, vaguely knowledgeable participants in an idea system (a social construction) that promotes a version of "the good life." Schools teach us an acceptable version of "human nature" that includes—along with reading, math, and computer skills—more subtle beliefs about mating rituals, status signaling, competition, the nuclear family, and concepts of success and failure.

What we don't learn is other ways to think about these things. When do we ever see that there are other beliefs possible? How often are students really encouraged in school to challenge beliefs they don't agree with? Instead, "Will this be on the test?" is the cliché question that reflects what the school assembly line teaches. We live our lives in terms of passing test after test that someone else has devised, and we are often blind to the test of our own lived experience.

Time, Energy, Contemplation

The easy way is to just keep suffering: to "do what we've always done" (or what our family or tribe have always done). This means that on some level, we accept the story that fear, frustration, and anger are part of life caused by forces acting on us. Lizzie makes me angry, for example. But it's not my fault; I have the correct beliefs. On some level or other, I'm rationalizing the frustrating nature of our relationship as "human nature."

Whenever we choose to "ride it out" because it seems easier, or we don't want to rock the boat, or any other rationalizations that have at their core the belief that "it's just human nature," we need to ask, "Which human nature?" Inuit human nature? Chinese human nature? Australian Aborigine human nature? German human nature circa 1938? Christ-consciousness human nature?

Socrates wanted each of us individually to look hard at fairness and decency, at hypocrisy and manipulation, and he was endlessly interested in how people rationalized selfishness and ignorance based on tribal beliefs, while fearing real education that taught debate. If you don't stop and examine—debate with yourself—why you're not getting what you think you want or

1. Do You Examine Your Life?

why you are angry and frustrated, you're missing out on the real key to "human nature": that is, humans can look at their beliefs and change them. We don't have to live in frustration, anger, or fear. We can grow toward love.

This kind of examination has moved me to know myself and my sister better. By seeing us for who we are, I can love and understand her better.

The key takeaway here is that if you are going to examine your life, you will need to know and recognize your habits. You'll need some kind of practice to address those habits, and there are many varieties available—I recommend meditation because it's free and you don't need a live teacher in the beginning. Find a style that you like, and if you don't know a style you like, go to Google or Ecosia (a new search engine that plants trees every time you click), plug in meditation styles, and you'll have a choice of about 65,900,000. Or simply start with the easy technique I recommend in the second chapter. It doesn't really matter what style it is because at the end of the day most meditation practice is trying to do the same thing: calm down our thinking mind so we can be more present and allow us to connect to the flow of positive energy in the universe. Are you taking the time and energy to contemplate your habits and maybe recognize yourself outside who your tribe wants you to be or who you feel you must be? Give yourself the opportunity to examine your life and reorganize your fearful experiences and emotions into a more open, honest, humble, and caring attitude.

Sweat This Out

In your notebook, jot down the one relationship in your life you know is unsatisfying. What is the underlying fear you feel when it comes to this person?

Without making a big deal about it, engage that person with the intent to create an *agreement*. It should be more than agreeing about the weather; see if you can find something you care about and figure out a way to get to an agreement with this other person. You will have to examine your life and your belief system and be willing to dig deep enough to possibly feel some discomfort and maybe even admit you're wrong on some ideas.

Good luck. Don't give up!

2. HOW DO YOU CREATE MORE PEACE IN YOUR LIFE?

Assume for the moment that peace is a good thing. When you feel peaceful, you're healthier, those around you feel calm and playful, and you create a sense of stability and confidence for those who deal with you.

However, many of us find ourselves in DRAMA. We believe we want a peaceful, playful, creative life, yet we feel anxious, angry with co-workers, frustrated that our spouse doesn't understand us, our kids are rebellious twerps who don't appreciate what we've sacrificed. It's hard to feel peaceful when you're under attack. And yet, how much of the attack is a circumstance that we have stoked in some way or another, possibly not even consciously. If you want to move toward peace, you'll need to let go of some habits and expectations and redirect a part of your life so it generates a sense of inner peace to draw from on a daily basis.

> I'm talking to the owner in a high-end fashion boutique about the merits of money and peace and how it manifests in our lives. She's putting a price tag on the new $750 Nikes that just came out of the box.
> "$750 for a pair of Nikes. Sounds a little high," I say.
> "People are really happy with these shoes," she responds.
> "Can I run seven hundred dollars' worth faster in these?"

27 QUESTIONS TO MAKE YOU SWEAT

"It's a fashion statement. It makes them happy."
"I guess money does buy pretty much anything."
"It's not all about money. Money can't buy everything."
"Actually, money can buy pretty much anything."
"What are you talking about? It can't buy health," she answers.
"What are you talking about? Of course it can. You can have a live-in vegan raw chef in your home. You can have a personal trainer every day, you can have a massage therapist on staff."
"You can still get cancer."
"Anyone can still get cancer, but with tons of bread you can definitely make much healthier lifestyle choices."
"You can't buy love."
"Well ... yes, you cannot buy deep true soulmate love. But having tons of money can certainly buy you versions of love. Just look around this community."
"I know plenty of miserable rich people," she says.
"I never said money buys peace of mind."
"You said money buys almost everything."
"Yeah, it does buy almost everything. But there is one thing money can't buy."
"What's that?"
"You can't pay someone to meditate for you."

I have a poster in my room to remind me of what I really want in life. It says, "Enlightenment is being aware of every breath." I'm not there yet, but I know I want to be more "enlightened" in the sense that I'm making choices in life and choosing to breathe, choosing love in all my relationships, business decisions, family interactions, even when I go shopping at the grocery store. When I drift into fear, it's usually when I'm running late, or I'm anxious

2. How Do You Create More Peace in Your Life?

about friends or finances, and I don't take the time to be with even simple acts like buying soup or being pleasant to someone waiting on me. If that sounds like something you can relate to—if you'd like to feel less fear and more peace—what can you do every day to ensure that you're feeding from that peaceful energy source?

Peace Takes Practice

How do we get to more peace? I'm asking you to agree with the idea that it takes practice; peace doesn't just happen. It's easier to fear. But peace is like playing a musical instrument; it takes practice, daily practice. And peace doesn't have to be mysterious; it can be as simple as turning your attention to what peace feels like. There are many roads to peace; I have chosen the path of meditation. You can start really simply doing anapana meditation a few minutes a day. In anapana you close your eyes and breath in normally and focus on your in-breath and then exhale and focus on your out breath. It's that simple. Breathe in, pay attention to the incoming breath, breathe out, pay attention to the outgoing breath. It's certainly not the only way, and it may not be for you, but it is a great place to start to gain control of your wandering mind.

I've been meditating for almost twenty-five years now. When I started, I didn't have a teacher or a method. I had been reading lots of books by Ram Dass (aka Richard Alpert), and in one of them he shared that he had received a mantra from his guru. Even though you're supposed to get a mantra from a live guru, I didn't have one at the time (nor do I now), so I figured if it was good enough for Ram, it would be good enough for me. I continued with that mantra for a few years until I learned Vipassana meditation, which I have been practicing ever since.

Vipassana is a form of meditation taught by the Buddha. I love it for two reasons: first, there is no dogma attached to it, and second, it's all about observing the sensations in your body and not reacting. You learn to obverse both pleasant and difficult sensations with the same measure of calm.

Being spiritual is recognizing the idea that we are essentially a spirit housed in a physical body, and feeling our connection to that spirit is our top priority. Our soul or spirit is the essence of who we are, and the closer we get to the essence of our soul, the more spiritual we become. We recognize a spiritual path in people by the qualities that come about as a by-product of focusing on the spirit: trust, honesty, gentleness, tolerance, patience, mercy, humor, generosity, gratitude, joy, defenselessness, and open-mindedness.

The less we pay attention to our soul, the less our activities reflect a spiritual reality. When honesty, tolerance, patience, mercy, and the rest of the qualities inherent in a spiritual life are not given top priority in our focus and awareness, then competition, envy, guilt, dishonesty and all other manifestations of fear take that top spot in our consciousness. The choice is always ours to make. Meditation is a tool that can help us stay focused on those positive life affirming qualities that make us feel better.

There is a Buddhist saying: "Everything is nothing, and nothing is everything." Getting inside this Buddhist riddle is a step toward understanding spiritual practice. At first glance, it may appear to be contradictory and confusing. Everything is emptiness or the Great Void or sacred silence or eternal peace or Nirvana, what some may experience as Nothing. That same Nothing is where Everything meaningful resides; joy, happiness, peace, love, harmony, patience, and all the other qualities that

2. How Do You Create More Peace in Your Life?

make our heart sing. The ability to tap into that universal field of energy, the Great Void, sacred silence, the universal flow of energy, God, the Now, whatever we call it, is good for the soul. The path we choose that directs us into that energy field doesn't really matter. What matters is that we're making the effort to be in that space every day and tapping into the giant power station inside our heart and mind.

We're all connected to the same energy in the universe, and as we spend more and more time bathing in that quiet energy, something happens. It's kind of a mystery, and at one level you could say that nothing happens. But each day that we do our spiritual practice, we're spending time in that mystical, universal ocean of energy where everything is possible—the space we call the present moment. As we spend more and more time there, our vibration, our consciousness, our soul all change. It's slow, it's gradual, and we can't see it happening, but we're moving in the direction of oneness, where we start to feel our connection to all people and begin to understand that when we hurt anyone, we're really hurting ourselves.

Throughout the ages, all the great spiritual masters have spoken about a path that begins to unravel the great mystery of consciousness and the path back home (or forward, depending on how you want to see time) toward our true self. We recognize a spiritual path in people by the qualities that come about as a by-product of focusing on the spirit, the ones we just spoke about.

Dressing in holy robes is completely inconsequential when it comes to embracing any of those qualities, but many are easily fooled by the outer display of holiness. This brings to mind one of the most profound lessons our grade school teachers tried to instill in us: don't judge a book by its cover. It's a lesson we still struggle with as adults.

27 QUESTIONS TO MAKE YOU SWEAT

I'm a firm believer in challenging the holy men and women we may encounter in our lives. If their claims are sincere, they'll be able to answer any inquiry with the utmost of patience, tolerance, and humility. And if they're incapable of responding in that light, that's our signal that they're just pretending and pontificating.

The easiest way to begin your spiritual journey is to shut up and sit down. The more spiritual way of saying this is to explore some kind of meditation practice. When you sit in silent meditation, you have a chance to step back from the inner drama inside and observe. You get a chance to hear the repetitive tapes that keep you mired in the anxious, frantic, scared space where most of us spend way too much time. Meditation can invoke a deep sense of calm and clarity, but it can also be quite challenging at the start. At first the idea that sitting in silence can be deafeningly loud makes no sense. But once you try it for more than two days, you'll understand why so many people give up and think, *I can't do this, it's much too hard. I'm freaking out, I just can't handle the hellish silence.* I'm done. But like anything worthwhile, you need to slog through the pain and have faith in the process. It's only through constant and continued practice that the mind learns to calm itself. I like to think of my morning and evening meditation as plugging into my peace and love power source, just like plugging an electric car into the electrical outlet.

Meditation and Medication

As time goes by, you observe the patterns of thought that keep you trapped in your melodramas and have a chance to change them. Through the discipline of sitting every day, you learn that you don't need to be so attached to your thoughts anymore. It's

2. How Do You Create More Peace in Your Life?

not an overnight cure, however, and in today's "I need everything yesterday" mindset, meditation often gets put on the back burner—replaced with the more immediate cure of medication. Medication certainly can play a pivotal role in improving one's life, but when it comes to mental health, it may not prove to be effective forever.

Both meditation and medication can be helpful for mental health, but there is one significant difference between them. With meditation you need to do *all* of the work to heal. With medication you don't need to do *any* of the work to heal. The meditation route puts the responsibility squarely on your shoulders, while the medication route puts the responsibility on your "mental illness," which the medication is responsible for "healing."

It's understandable that people struggling with serious mental issues don't believe they have the energy to heal themselves. Yet we know that after surgery, the sooner you start the painful process of moving your weakened body, the quicker and safer you will heal. Why can't we instill that same vigor for work in our mental health healing that we expect in our physical health healing and make it mandatory that someone with mental issues at least try and meditate?

Whether it's meditation, the religion you were born into, or some way-out esoteric practice, choose a path that involves merging your soul with the divine in some way, a practice that brings you closer to the state of oneness where you and your brother are united. It doesn't really matter what path you take, because eventually we all end up in the same place. As the great Kundalini Yoga Master Yogi Bhajan liked to say, "You can take a donkey or you can take the Concorde; it's up to you." The only question is how long do you want to wait until you're

27 QUESTIONS TO MAKE YOU SWEAT

having your morning, afternoon, and evening coffee with God? He's not going anywhere, so ostensibly you have all the time in the world. But now is the only time there will ever be!

Sweat This Out

This exercise comes in two parts:

1. Sit for five minutes without doing anything. If you think that sounds like what you've heard about meditation, you'd be right. But "meditation" can sound like there's something you're "supposed" to be "doing." Instead do nothing but breathe. If you find you must do something, count your breaths in tens. One inhale, one exhale, two inhales, two exhales, ten exhales and you start over. That's all. Time yourself for five minutes. Doing this simple exercise creates two mental states at once: awareness of breathing and letting go of expectations. Expectations are thoughts in our minds that keep us going from one thing to another throughout the day. Generally, expectations are good. However, by directing your mind to your breath, you are becoming mindful of only what is happening now; you are dropping your expectations. Over time, you become mindful of how much your expectations control you, when perhaps you should control them.

2. The second part of this exercise is to keep

2. How Do You Create More Peace in Your Life?

a short journal for the week. You don't have to write volumes, but you must write at least one paragraph about your experiences during the day. You can describe internal or external experiences; it makes no difference. What does make the difference is doing it. Notice what you've done, said, and accomplished that day. Watch how writing it down makes you feel. If you see yourself enjoying this moment of introspection, it's a gift you can give yourself every day. If you feel anxious or unhappy, note that down in your journal too. You may see that your emotions are connected to expectations; if so, note down those expectations without judging if they're good or bad, right or wrong. Use your journal to connect with your perspective, seeing what you're doing, noticing your pleasures and your pains. Just write them down.

3. WHAT MAKES YOU ANGRY?

Emotions have us; we don't have emotions. That's just to say that emotions precede our consciousness . . . and usually our control.

>At the end of his tennis lesson on a hot day in August, Mr. Klein and I were hydrating with fresh lemonade in the shade of the patio overlooking his personal tennis court. Mr. Klein was upset about the minimum wage. (This was sometime in the mid-nineties.)
>"It's going to bankrupt businesses all over our great country."
>"Mr. Klein, that's complete horseshit, and you know it. How can you say that?"
>"Because it's true. If you raise the minimum wage to ten dollars an hour, you will be putting thousands of small business owners out of business."
>"If ten dollars an hour is the minimum living wage, business owners can adjust all other costs accordingly."
>"That's ridiculous, Gregg—you don't know what you're saying."
>"It's basic economics. Whatever your minimum cost is in starting capital, you now include ten dollars an hour so employees can work one job for forty hours a week and survive. The present minimum wage forces people of all ages to work

two jobs."

"So you want to prevent thousands of people from starting small businesses?"

"Starting a business is a choice. No one is forced to start a business. My point is that if you expect to make a fair profit from your business, first calculate if it's doable while paying your employees a living wage. If you want to start a business, you have to plan on paying that wage. That would be moral and ethical. If your business plan depends on exploiting people, what is your business really worth? I'm not a big fan of exploiting people who are so desperate for work that they'll slave to enrich an owner who tucks away their efforts in profits."

"Gregg, I make my money understanding how business runs. Last I checked that wasn't your forte."

"Why are you insulting me? Because you have more money than I do? Does that make it right for you to resort to name-calling when you can't respond to a reasonable argument?"

"You began by calling my position 'horseshit,' if you recall."

"Well, it makes me angry when the average worker can't make a living wage working forty hours a week. Why does it make you angry when they might?"

"I shouldn't have to sacrifice my opportunity when market forces are the best way to determine wage costs."

"You know that modern markets are controlled more by capital than 'market forces.' You believe the only people that should have any say in economics are people that have already made millions of dollars—and you don't understand why that might make me angry?"

"When you've made your first million, come back and we can discuss this reasonably."

Mr. Klein and I were having a real conversation, but we

3. What Makes You Angry?

couldn't get to a place of peace because we were both locked in our anger. Therefore, nothing changed.

Economic ideas can make almost anyone angry. I'm angry because I think it's unjust that workers don't get paid enough to live on. Mr. Klein is angry because he thinks workers should be paid solely on market forces. Obviously, we take our beliefs very seriously and can't agree. The fact that we get angry is a cue to how important these ideas are to us. We both see our positions in terms of moral right and wrong. And the truth is, this is an argument worth having out loud and in public. My moral position on this is based on the idea of sharing enough of the wealth so the workers can live without being on the verge of financial collapse at every turn. Mr. Klein's idea is that anyone who wants to be a millionaire should be able to play the market to get there.

Some anger is worth having because it can be the fuel for fighting injustices like sexism, racism, environmental degradation, bombing helpless people in foreign countries, and so on—all good reasons to be angry. I think that's a pretty clear moral argument, and I also think that having the argument, getting angry enough to support political candidates, going out and educating others—even if the Mr. Kleins of the world are resistant to learning anything—is a chance to spend angry energy in a positive way.

So that's part of the issue. On the other hand, I lose my shit when I get behind a slow driver. That idiot mofo is *wasting my time and gas*. I usually am going someplace on schedule. Driving 25 mph is less economical than 35. Time and gas are money, you idiot! I'm afraid I'll be late. I'm afraid of wasting money on gas. Even if I'm coming home at night and I'm not going to be late, I still get pissed off behind a slow driver. I still can't stand the thought of wasting time, wasting my life, behind some dimwit who doesn't realize there are other drivers in the world. Like me. Behind you, dimwit!

I guess I don't really know what it is on the deepest level that makes me so crazy about having to slow down for another driver. Is it that I don't want another person to have power over me? Am I really afraid that I've already wasted my life and the time to make up for it could be wasted, too, by the few extra minutes this drive will take me? Is it that I want to control my speed my way? In the end, I desperately want to feel like I'm controlling my destiny and mistaking the fact that being behind this slowpoke is a situation over which I have no power.

This kind of anger gets me nothing except closer to a coronary. Yet I do it over and over again. What's with that? I'm still working on it. What would happen if I didn't get pissed behind the Crown Vicky driving 23 mph in a 30 mph zone? What if I took a breath and said, "OK, I'll be a couple minutes late for an appointment. Everyone understands traffic."

Or "I really need to leave earlier."

Or what if I just enjoyed the ride?

So, this is how I'm processing my anger. I'm noticing what happens when I get angry: What's the trigger? What do I do? And I'm asking myself the question: Is this necessary? Does getting angry change anything? And if it doesn't, the next question is: What am I afraid of?

Anger is one of the most powerful emotions we have, and learning how to express it in a healthy way is not only one of the most charitable things we can do for those around us but also one of the most important mental health steps we can take for ourselves.

How do we express anger in a healthy way? With difficulty!

3. What Makes You Angry?

There are multiple ways of expressing anger, but the two most popular methods most of us learn as children are:

- repress our anger at all costs and do our best not to rock the boat
- mirror the behavior we've observed in a parent or caretaker with a rage issue

If we want to live with some sense of peace, we need to find the balance between keeping everything bottled up inside and freaking out and raging at the world. This requires work.

Speaking loudly and passionately while you're fighting with your significant other without scaring them off and making them feel bad requires the disciplined, focused work of being mindful, slowing down, breathing, and paying attention to what the other person is saying. Far too often when we're screaming and ranting at our partners, we're so busy paying attention to our own hurts and pains that we completely forget about their feelings.

It takes practice to be mindful when you get pissed off at your boyfriend for being late or your kids for being lazy or your mother for her incessant nagging. But if learning to express your anger in a healthy way that doesn't repress the anger and at the same time doesn't scare off whomever you're communicating with at the time is important to you, then keep practicing and keep the faith that in time you will be able to feel more love for the people in your life that annoy you.

Sweat This Out

In your notebook, make a list from one to ten. Think about the past week and note down when you were angry. For the next two days, keep track of your anger events. They can happen anytime: watching the news on TV; talking to your mom on the phone; waiting in line; or watching your favorite team lose ("Damn the refs!"). What about your significant other—what did she or he do that irritated you so much that you got angry?

Note down what happened when you felt angry. How did your body feel? Where did your turn your attention?

Did you shout at the TV or at _____?

Did you sulk? She: "What's wrong?" Me: "Nothing. I'm fine." She: "You're awfully quiet." Me: "I'm just thinking, that's all." (She knows that pisses me off. Why does she always do it?)

Did you throw your beer at the third baseman?

Did you plot some way to get back at the person who angered you?

As you note what triggered you, write down exactly what happened. After your angry behavior, what happened to your body? After you're angry, how do you feel?

Imagine letting your anger play out completely, with no restraint. What kind of a murderous, shriek-fest temper tantrum would that be?

Or . . .

3. What Makes You Angry?

If you were to find the place of love in the situation, what would that look like? Would it be as easy as enjoying the anger ride? The important part of this is to recognize the progression of anger from a stimulus to an angry response, and then be aware of what your angry response does to your body.

Finally, try to see yourself several minutes before the anger emerges. What triggered it? Is it possible that your anger was triggered by something earlier in your life? Possibly from another relationship with a bad power dynamic? Are work, family, and sex overlapping? Or does some habit set you up to be angry? Is it possible that you habitually don't plan for five minutes of extra driving time when you leave so you can have your road rage?

Fair warning: there are powerful emotions behind the anger. It's not easy. Take a look.

4. HOW DO YOU SPEND YOUR TIME?

Have you ever really looked at the hours you spend on the various things you do? Time is like money; you have it, and you spend it. And what you buy with your time tells you who you are. To help see who you really are, let's look at a typical month and see how you spend your time bank account. There's time at your job, which is different from time spent going to or coming from your job; there's time spent sleeping and eating, shopping and bathing, brushing your teeth.... Often you'll find yourself doing two things at once. You might spend the same time talking on the phone as you do driving to work.

In order to answer this question, come up with some definite categories you devote time to and then note down how many hours you spend per each activity in a month. Think of a "typical" month, not December or other holiday or vacation periods. During a four-week period, you have 672 hours. If you spend a total of thirty hours eating each week, that's 120 hours a month. As you add up all your activities, your totals (including the overlaps) will probably exceed 672. If you eat with your partner once a day for an hour (twenty-eight hours a month), count those hours both in "Eating" and "Partner." Even though you'll have more than 672 hours, you'll have total quantities in each category, and you'll see how you spend your time.

Are you ready? It's easy! Your life involves many complex

27 QUESTIONS TO MAKE YOU SWEAT

responsibilities and relationships, but don't fret. No one will check your homework. Just fill in your monthly numbers on this chart:

A. Sleep. (if you sleep with your partner, count only the time you're both awake together in bed.) Hours per month: _____ (probably just above or below 200-240 hours)

B. Eating. Hours per month: _____

C. Preparing food. Hours per month: _____

D. Occupation. Whatever you do as a job or vocation, whether or not it involves making money. Include activities such as business reading or other job-essential education; also include job-specific relationship maintenance such as client dinners, phone or email schmoozing, website maintenance, etc.) Hours per month: _____

E. Chores. Include all necessary housekeeping: cleaning, shopping for food, washing dishes and clothes, yard work, taking out the trash. Hours per month: _____

F. Religion. Your religious practice or engagement with religious organizations. Hours per month: _____

G. Health. Taking care of your physical health: going to the gym, seeing doctors, taking the time to use the stairs, walking, etc. Hours per month: _____

H. Money management. Paying bills, banking, managing credit cards, investments, etc. Hours per month: _____

I. Maintaining your physical property. Fixing the sink, landscaping, staining the deck, etc. Hours per month: ____

4. How Do You Spend Your Time?

J. Hobbies. Activities you do for fun or curiosity or self-exploration: watercolor painting; playing in an eighties band; detailing and waxing your '56 T-bird; changing the inks in your fountain pen collection; knitting; and if you see food, cooking, and gardening as hobbies as well as essential to survival, count them twice. Hours per month: _____

K. Time spent in active collaboration with your spouse, significant other, or life partner/lover in relationship and family responsibilities. Hours per month: _____

L. Pleasure time spent with your significant other. Going to movies, socializing with other adults, having sex, watching TV—adult playtime. Hours per month: _____

M. Taking care of mental health. Therapy, meditation, yoga, etc. Hours per month: _____

N. Raising children. Time-consuming, dedicated actions (could include meal prep) that you do as an individual (as opposed to item K). Hours per month: _____

O. Making life work better for others: family, friends, community groups. Hours per month: _____

P. Going on adventures or taking risks that are unique and thrilling. Hours per month: _____

Q. Service to your country or other government, civic, or educational institutions. (This counts in two categories if you're a fireman or a schoolteacher, etc., or if the government or other humanistic organization signs your paycheck.) Hours per month: _____

27 QUESTIONS TO MAKE YOU SWEAT

R. Shopping for things that aren't necessities at *brick-and-mortar stores* (not online). Hours per month: _____

S. Playing with media entertainments. Such things as online shopping, streaming, social media, gambling, watching television including sports, Snapchat, Instagram, videogames, reading for pleasure, going to the movies, watching pornography. Hours per month: _____

T. Travel time. No matter where you're going, whether to work, to pick up the kid at soccer or ballet, or to the doctor or grocery store. Include business travel to distant locations (not vacations). Hours per month: _____

Now that you have your monthly totals, take a moment to admire yourself for being so organized and taking this time to appreciate the many levels of your life. Most people never do this in their entire lives. (Listen for the applause!)

So now, let's compare your totals.

In the space below, list in the order of most hours to least, all your time spent. You might want to use a cue word to remind you what those hours are for ("168 hrs sleep," for instance, will be the "Most" category for most people).

Most hours spent (1) to least hours spent (20)
Suggestion: Sleep (for most people, 8hrs/30 days, is the most time spent, 240 hrs)
Suggestion: occupation (8hrs/20 days is second, 160 hrs)

Now, look at the numbers of hours; this reflects your "spending" of your time. The stuff at the top is what's most important to you. The stuff at the bottom doesn't matter that much.

4. How Do You Spend Your Time?

Are the priorities of your beliefs in line with your priorities of action?

Here's another system you can use to get a picture of your time-spending.

Pencil in one of the following WORDS for each activity:

LOVE: things you love to do

OK: things you are OK with doing, but it's not a love thing

HOT and COLD: sometimes this is great, sometimes not so much, sometimes you'd rather not

SACRIFICE: things you feel you must do, and the payoff is that your efforts improve you, someone else, or go toward a greater purpose. Sometimes doing this can feel like a pure obligation; yet afterward, you're glad you soldiered through it.

RESENTMENT: shit you gotta do that gives you a very irritated emotional charge. There are degrees of resentment in life, but any resentment always makes doing something an unpleasant experience. This category is often the result of a slow buildup of circumstances.

For example:

Sleep 278 hours—For most people, sleep is a LOVE.

Occupation 160 hours—I do my job only because it supports my family: SACRIFICE or I get some satisfaction from my job's challenges, but there's a lot of paperwork that I could do without: OK

Childcare 180 hours—Consider a mother of two very young children: given her choice, she might not be changing diapers, feeding, washing, cleaning up after, driving to pediatrician, etc.; her babies are beautiful, wonderful playmates for maybe twenty or thirty hours of that 180: HOT COLD

Going to the gym—It's not always fun, but it can be: HOT COLD

RESENTMENT is possibly the trickiest category because it's so subjective, and resentment is a complicated emotion—part anger, part fear, part discomfort—and it makes you passive. It could be disguised in your mind as SACRIFICE, but in truth, you hate it.

Boredom is often a pretty good indicator of resentment—for instance, committee meetings you must attend but have no great interest in. Resentments sap our energy and concentration.

Be brutally honest. Remember, no one will check your work. How much of your time is spent loving or even liking what you're doing, and how much is . . . ?

Good work!

Here's the big payoff: You are "spending" your time. It's like money in many ways. Where does your time-cashflow go?

How much do you consciously control?

What part of *your* time do others control?

The numbers are *who you are right now, baby.*

And the numbers don't lie.

5. HOW DO YOUR INSECURITIES HOLD YOU BACK?

In the Sphere of Fear, people say, "No one respects me. I've got to prove myself all the time. Everyone competes with me. I can tell by their attitude they are criticizing me. I have to show them."
In the Circle of Love, people play. They see life as a game to engage with and learn from. Other people's judgments are other people's judgments. If someone is better at doing something than you, that's an opportunity to learn. If you're confident and calm within, you're in the Circle of Love, and you look for ways to cooperate with others, play with them, and draw them into your Circle.

> *I had just gotten up from my drums and was leaving the bandstand in the Mexican restaurant with our bass player Jonas.*
> *"Good set, Gregg. You sounded great."*
> *"Thanks, Jonas." Jonas and I had been "in the pocket" all night long.*
> *I spotted Lena—we were married then—in the back of the room. She seemed distracted.*
> *"How was it, baby?" I was feeling good, hoping she'd heard that solid bottom.*
> *"It was okay," she replied.*
> *"Okay?"*
> *"Yeah, it was pretty good."*

27 QUESTIONS TO MAKE YOU SWEAT

"Was I playing too loud?"
"You sounded good."
"But was I too loud?"
"Gregg, the band sounded good—relax."
"I know, Jonas is amazing. The guy was killing it."
"Yeah, he's really good."
"How was my solo in 'Mr P.C.'?"
"It was good."
"You don't sound that enthused."
"Gregg, what's your problem? You know how to play... relax."
"I know, but these guys are really good."
"Yeah, but you're really good. What's up with you? You're acting like you've never played jazz before."
"Not with guys at this level."
"What are you talking about? You play with Luke all the time."
I took a seat next to Lena, but after a few minutes, I just couldn't let it go.
"It really sounded good—no joke?"

I've always been insecure around top-tier jazz musicians. Maybe it's silly, but I have always been in awe of cats who can really play. Movie stars, meh; sports stars, pretty cool; rock stars, awesome; but Jazz stars—the shit! These are superheroes. There are just a few of them on the planet, and hearing them play is like a religious experience for me. It's otherworldly. When I hear these true masters play, I hear so much that surprises me, and I wish I could do what they do. But honestly, they seem so superhuman to me that I sometimes get queasy and insecure when I'm around them.

If I have a gig with a really top player, I find myself feeling afraid that I'm not good enough, so I start thinking that's what

5. How Do Your Insecurities Hold You Back?

they think. I get anxious and feel like I have to compete to show them—but, yo, music is not competition; that's why they call it "playing." My anxiety to prove myself makes me tighten up, but the drummer needs to stay loose. My fear and insecurity make me rush, and I lose my feeling for the pocket (the strong, steady, rhythmic groove which is the drummer's first priority). My haste to prove what a great drummer I am makes me paradiddle myself into being a worse musician and takes all the pleasure out of playing.

I haven't asked, but when I was younger, it might have made me hard to work with.

Ouch.

However, a number of years ago, my friend Martha did what true friends do: she told me I needed to be honest with myself.

"Look, dumb shit," she said (Martha's a very direct person), "music is a choice for everyone. You're good. Relax. You got the gig because they like your playing. But if you treat a gig like a competition, no one will like playing with you. Your worries about 'how good am I?' are all in your head."

Message received. Thank you, Martha.

I'm a big believer that talking about our insecurities is the first step to dismantle them. When we fear that something's wrong, it's difficult to look inside, and fear creates confusion. I was insecure about my playing. I was putting "professional" goals on myself that, as Martha observed, were too unrealistic. Those performative goals meant I had to prove I was a "professional musician" all the time, so I practiced obsessively, I taught, I gigged as much as possible, and was a little too eager to work with the really good players. That insecurity came off as desperation and competition. As Martha observed: "Gregg, you're so tight, I could bounce a quarter off your asshole." She was right. It was all about proving I was great, not the here-and-now musical collaboration.

I didn't like hearing that, but up on the bandstand, I could feel myself—my face, my body—working too hard at *performing*. To put it mildly: it wasn't a swinging feeling. My need to prove myself was making me not fun—not fun for me, not fun for my friends, and not fun to work with.

One thing was really clear: I needed to stop trying so damn hard to be impressive and rediscover why I was playing in the first place. As I began the process of consciously letting go of *proving myself* to others, I felt really exposed and vulnerable. Straining had become part of my act, so I had to get comfortable just playing and not straining. I had to give up Type-A stressing, and when I did, I discovered that even if I didn't spend the entire day practicing, I could still play some killer sets in the evening. And that the killer part would emerge from listening, not stressing. It required letting go of the fear that I wasn't good enough—much of this coming from my past—and *play* with others. Then I could realistically see how people were reacting, and we could play cooperatively.

I started taking only the gigs I really wanted to play. I got another job—teaching tennis again, which I'm also good at, but I don't obsess over—and it was almost like magic. People started to comment about the look of joy on my face when I was gigging. Duh! I was having fun. The truth was I could play professionally and just relax, and that good solid pocket could hold anyone. I just had to *play with the band*, not striving to prove I belonged in the band in the first place.

Martha helped me acknowledge my insecurities. As I began relaxing more, I began a process that helped me realize how events in my past had trained that anxious response; I had the

5. How Do Your Insecurities Hold You Back?

habit of insecurity and self-doubt. I began asking myself how I could release my habitual insecurities. How would I feel if I wasn't trying to prove something? Could I just be me in the moment? I saw that if I could love what I do, then I would love me, and that would be enough.

That's easy to say, not so easy to do. At some level, call it a conditioned response, my insecurities always seemed "logical," maybe even comfortable. My father had conditioned me by his constant disapproval that it was "logical" for me to work obsessively to be any good. "You have to try harder, Gregg. How will you ever be any good, if you don't try harder?"

Today, I can see that his "lessons" about my musicianship came from his own insecurities. He had wanted to be a singer, but in the professional world, he hadn't been good enough. The story he told himself was that he had the talent, but he hadn't tried hard enough. You can see that he thought he was helping me, but instead he gave me his insecurity.

In the process of learning to enjoy my own talent—which is real and maybe inherited from my dad—I've learned sympathy for my dad as well. His essential insecurity made him try to manipulate other people to make himself look and feel good. He didn't have the courage or the calmness to stop and *honestly observe* himself. Every time he told me that I wasn't "good enough," he was repeating his own judgment of his singing career. In some twisted way, he may have been trying to save me from the pain he felt in failing.

In some ways, my dad was the poster boy for how insecurity can hold you back. He didn't trust himself, and his insecurity was so powerful that he stressed over everything. He saw the world as he saw himself, so he didn't trust his kids to be good enough or his wife to be a cooperative partner. He tried to control us all into "performing" success for him, instead of accepting his children who just wanted to play with dad. When Martha said, "Cut the shit. You're making yourself crazy," I realized I was still performing for Dad.

Our insecurities are, for the most part, just bad memories that have turned into habits of thought. And yes, they will drive us crazy if we can't honestly see them and own them. That's where Martha came in. She had no personal investment except that she was my friend. When I'd bitch about how anxious and stressed I felt about not having "good enough gigs" because I feared I wasn't a "good enough player," she could see that my complaints weren't an accurate understanding of what was true. The stress was polluting my playing. She helped me see that I was using "good enough" to make myself miserable when I had an opportunity to loosen up and swing.

Here's a key thing: sometimes thinking you're not good enough is, in fact, a reality. Sure, I might want to be an astronaut, but honey, that ship has sailed. I'm not getting there from here. That's just testing reality. Other times, the habit of self-doubt is what prevents us from an achievement or even a relationship we're ready for. To get a better handle on reality, I listened to Martha because she's a hard-ass and a truth-teller, and I knew she wouldn't candy-coat anything to make me feel better. It hurt to hear her assessment, but when it sunk in, I knew she confirmed the truth of my experience. I was performing out of insecurity, fearful that I wasn't good enough. I had to see that my habit of trying really hard was, in fact, just anxiety.

I felt different when I was just drumming for me. It's a lot easier to blame others—"Those assholes just don't see how great I am"—when we fail, but blaming others pretty much guarantees you'll wind up like my dad: endlessly unhappy with yourself. But

5. How Do Your Insecurities Hold You Back?

if you enlist others to help you, if you're willing to honestly own that you might be the real problem and not blame others (a step that takes courage), it shifts the power from others to you. This gives you the power to see and change your insecurities.

Sweat This Out

Step one: At the top of the page, write "Fears, Anxieties, and Insecurities." Number your page from one to ten. Jot down situations, activities, responsibilities, and relationship interactions that make you anxious or fearful, or that frustrate you.

Money? Love? Parents or parenting? Arriving on time? Holidays? Job?

Write down everything that comes to mind, even the dumbest things. This is for you, not for anyone else.

Step two: Pick one activity that makes you feel anxious, stressed, or angry. Those are the signs of insecurity. Sometimes we actually should be insecure to protect ourselves, but not every time.

Pick an anxiety that you're aware most other people can handle. Fear of flying? Anxiety with money or organizing? Difficulty with strangers?

Find a private time to ask one of your friends or one of your family members to *just listen* as you tell them about how you feel in that situation.

"Just listen" is important. You're not asking for judgment or help; you just want them to listen without advising or trying to make you feel better.

Try to be as honest as possible even if you can't get deeply into it. Just relaying your exact feelings to another person is a giant step.

Break off before either of you gives in to the temptation to fix the problem.

It's only one small insecurity, yet if you actually do this exercise, you take a step toward owning your feelings. There's power in ownership. The key is trying!

6. HOW DOES IT FEEL WHEN YOU LIE?

Except for a very few human beings who have achieved deep self-awareness—and with it a kind of enlightened fearlessness—the rest of humanity tells lies every day. Or, if lying sounds too harsh, we tell untruths. This is a psychologically provable fact. We lie with inaccuracies; we lie by omitting details; we lie from laziness. But the truth behind lying is that we do it—sometimes unconsciously—to avoid pain and experience pleasure. We have an *idea* about what we want or what we deserve, and we bend what we say to get that idea. But how does it feel?

In the sphere of fear, we're so locked into what we want, we tell untruths to bend reality to suit those wants. In the circle of love, we don't need to protect our ideas, but instead we are willing to be vulnerable and responsible in the truth of the moment.

I was fifteen years old, strolling out of the kitchen with a toasted bagel in my hand on the way to my favorite place on the couch, my go-to spot after a long day at school, ready to chill and groove on tunes. But as I stepped into the living room, I saw a big, empty room.

Something was waaay wrong. I yelled, "Dad, where did the living room furniture go?"

His voice came down the stairs just ahead of his steps. "Don't worry about it, Gregg; it'll be back soon."

"Back from where?"

"My friend Jim is borrowing it for a little while."

"Borrowing our living room furniture? Who borrows living room furniture?"

"Gregg it's not your concern. It will be back soon enough."

"Dad, people like Jim don't borrow living room furniture. He lives in a huge house. He has his own furniture."

"He's going through a tough time, and I'm helping him out."

"Wait. Does he still live in the same house? Did it burn down or something?"

"Enough, Gregg. Jim has the living room furniture for now. When he gets his own, we'll get it back."

"When does he plan on getting his own?"

"There's plenty of furniture in the house, Gregg. You'll survive without a living room couch, for God's sake. It's not that big a deal."

"This is an empty room, Dad. It feels like kind of a big deal."

It was obvious my dad was lying. I never found out for sure, but if I had a million dollars to bet, I'd say he'd pawned the entire living room. From the time I was in middle school, gradually our lives had fewer things, and my dad stopped going to the door or answering the phone, telling us to say he was out of town on business.

I never felt right when I lied to whoever was calling. But I felt like I *had to lie* . . . because my father asked me to, to protect him, and to protect myself and the family. The only chance I had of getting the couch back was hoping that the lies would work out. And of course, once the couch was gone—and it was a fucking great couch—it was gone forever.

Somewhere in my head, I could put all the blame on my dad: he told me to lie; therefore, it was his lie. Plus, I didn't want to

6. How Does It Feel When You Lie?

face the consequences of not doing what he wanted. At the time, I didn't really consider that I had another option.

But I hated that feeling. I felt like I wasn't really me when I "had to" lie.

As I grew up, I resolved to tell the truth about myself and my life as well I was able. I wanted to avoid that dirty, confused feeling that came with giving manipulative, incorrect, or incomplete information.

So, yeah, I think I can forgive myself for *those* lies.

But I think it reveals the problem of lying more generally. When we lie, it "feels" wrong. The truth of our experience isn't lining up with what we're saying or what we avoid saying. In our minds, it can feel as though "I don't have a choice," and at the same time as though "It's not my fault." We rationalize this disjointed thinking because we think we want what's not true. Umm . . . does that sound like a good idea?

When we lie, we're like children who are, in some ways, powerless to tell the truth. Like I was. As children, we're dominated by someone else. We have to do the dirty work for an idea of power and in the process, we sell out our own actual, honest power.

Thinking about these things provides a model for recognizing how the lie feels so we can catch ourselves when we do it. Most of us will justify or rationalize our lies, like I did when I tried to cooperate with my dad in hopes of getting the couch back. In some way, we imagine lying must be the right thing to do, using those feelings of "I don't have a choice" and/or "It's not my fault."

If you lie to your boss to avoid getting fired, you might tell yourself, "It's not my fault. I have to keep my job. Everybody makes mistakes . . ."

If you lie to your wife about being attracted to another

woman, you might feel as though you don't have a choice; you tell yourself she's so insecure that she couldn't handle it.

If you lie to your parents about your boyfriend's religion, you can think *It's not my fault*—your parents are narrow-minded, and if you want to date him without endless conflict, you tell yourself, "I don't have a choice."

But as adults—if we're going to evolve as moral beings—those feelings are cues to how much we are afraid, and out of fear, how much we try to manipulate other people. Problem: in manipulating others, we give up a piece of who we really are. We imagine that, by lying, we're avoiding pain—but even if that's true, by avoiding pain now, we are likely creating pain in the future. Why? Because in the lie there is a seed of distrust: you don't trust someone else to fully understand you; you don't trust that someone will love you enough to understand you; most importantly, you don't trust *yourself* to be fully responsible. The seed of distrust can always grow, and nothing fertilizes it better than lies.

If we don't tune in to when we lie, it can become a habit. We can learn to comfort ourselves with lies, just to feel as though we're controlling some part of our lives. But with each successive lie, we become more and more frightened of allowing others to see us as we truly are, until eventually we've lost touch with our authentic self. What if the lie about your boyfriend's religion is what you always tell your parents and then you want to get married? Maybe you elope so they don't see any religion in the ceremony, but as time goes on, how many lies will you have to tell to keep them from knowing the truth? This isn't just an absurd example; it's an accurate way of projecting what inevitably will happen when the first lie is "successful," and then requires the next lie.

When we're faced with decisions about how to present the truth, preserving a comfortable status quo may be the lie that's

6. How Does It Feel When You Lie?

easy to tell. Hey, no religious problems in our family. Or there's something you think you want—a job, a sale, an attractive person's attention—and it's easy to lie, to manipulate the truth. And yet do you really want to get a job, a sale, a romantic relationship based on a lie? Will you have the strength to keep lying when the customers or lovers discover the lie? What do you say if they are furious with your manipulation? Of course, there are degrees. Getting a job based on the lie that you own twenty different three-piece suits is radically different than getting a job based on the lie that you speak three different languages.

Granted, the moment of truth can be difficult. If what comes out of my mouth is only what I "should" say to get what I think I need right now, that's the definition of a fear. I'm afraid to say who I really am; I'm afraid that my friend won't understand; I'm afraid a boss won't hire me; I'm afraid that the real me isn't attractive enough.

Here's the key question: When are we performing to manipulate others and when are we communicating the truth of our real feelings? They feel different. My father wanted me to lie to protect him. When I told those lies, I felt like I was performing, and it's that feeling of performance that has cued me to when I'm lying. Over time, though, it's become clear to me that all the "performing" I was doing was just living in fear, afraid that the real me wouldn't be loved.

I like to believe I tell the truth 95 percent of the time. I try to tell the whole truth except when doing so would be cruel or inappropriate.

"Do I really sound like an ignorant high school kid when I hang around with my boss and his wife?"

Clearly you'd be an idiot to say yes, so you tell a little lie: "No, you seem pretty comfortable." It's a way of telling a half-truth:

I believe in you and I want you to believe in yourself so I tell a little white lie to give you confidence. In some cases, saying the words that give the person what he or she needs or expresses the truth of your feelings over the truth of the circumstances is the most loving thing you can do. But the "little white lie" can be a slippery slope: if you're using it out of fear to protect yourself from behavior you know is inappropriate or wrong, then it's no longer a "little white lie."

When you tell your partner, "I took her straight home. We just stopped for gas for five minutes," when you actually stopped in a parking lot for fifteen minutes to fool around, that's a completely different kind of "little white lie" than saying "You seemed pretty comfortable" after a dinner party where your partner was clearly nervous and anxious. The second is said to help build a person's confidence and self-esteem, while the other is said to protect yourself from behavior you don't feel good about.

As I've struggled to be happy and have meaningful and balanced relationships, I've learned to trust my truth because that's the foundation of real love. I have to trust those I love with my actual feelings. I want to communicate what they need to know to understand my feelings, even if my feelings are my doubts, my uneasiness—those fears and even weird desires everyone has from time to time. I don't need to perform "nice talk" to make them think I'm normal, not the slightly eccentric person that, at our core, *we all are*.

The amazing thing about truth is that it benefits everyone. Even when we fear the result of telling the truth, it liberates an energy: the energy of trust. I trust myself to tell the truth, and that signals other people that they can tell their truth.

"Isn't Susan's dress hot?"

"Yeah, Susan's pretty sexy."

6. How Does It Feel When You Lie?

"I think Tommy's ass looks really cute in those jeans."

"Should I be jealous?"

When we tell the whole truth, we're being intimate, so there's no need to feel jealous.

It feels risky because so much of what the world tells us is that we *have to perform* normal behavior. Yet normal is often pretty boring, as well as a lie.

The best we can do to help the people in our lives tell the truth is to communicate as honestly as possible about ourselves and our beliefs, and to guard against sliding into the habit of telling others how we think they should think and feel.

Here is one of my favorite quotes from an unknown source:

Truth is like surgery; it hurts but it cures. A lie is like a painkiller. It gives instant relief, but its side effects can last forever. The surgery cures your physical body just like the truth cures/frees your emotional/spiritual body.

Telling the truth is like driving with your eyes open: it's always better than when they're closed.

Sweat This Out

For the next two days, carry your notebook around, and after every conversation you have, jot down a number from one to four on how honest you think you were during that interaction—one being total truth, two being half-truth, three being a performance, and four being complete manipulation. It will just take a moment and a bit of determination on your part.

Just before you go to sleep, take a look and see how you did during the day. Don't judge yourself—just notice your relationship with truth.

7. WHEN IS ENOUGH MONEY ENOUGH?

Your Happy Money: is it a steady income or a lump sum? If it's a lump sum, is it around a million dollars? Is it ten million? Are you imagining that that lump of ten mil is going to last you the rest of your life while you do . . . what? Go on permanent vacation?

If a steady income is your choice, what would that be? $1,200 a week after taxes? That's about the median earning rate for an American household of four.

Or do you think that $1,200 a week isn't anywhere nearly enough to pay the rent or mortgage, feed the kids, buy the groceries, and fuel the car? That's the Sphere of Fear. Would two thousand a week be the right amount to get you out of the Sphere of Fear?

Or is it possible that the more you have, the more you'll spend?

If it's true that the more you get, the more you spend, then you will use any amount of money to keep you in the Sphere of Fear; your habit of spending is controlling you. If you feel you constantly need more than you have, you are choosing to live in fear.

However, if you play the game of money in a way that allows you to have enough, then you have moved into the Circle of Love. You control your money, not feel like it controls you.

Mr. Klein and I had just hopped into his golf cart for our pre-lesson stroll around his thirty-acre estate. The rolling hills were emerald green, and the ponds were filled with quacking ducks.

27 QUESTIONS TO MAKE YOU SWEAT

"Why do you seem so happy today, Mr. Klein?"
"I made two million dollars today."
"Two million dollars in one day? You must have worked your ass off today."
"Yes, I did."
"I hope so. That's an insane amount of money." (And that's 1980's money—today it would be closer to four million).
"It's not that it's so much money; today I felt like I earned it, like I really was on my game. It felt like the old days."
"What do you mean 'the old days'?"
"When I first started, I was hungry. Every day was a new opportunity to make it happen, to go out there and fight, to struggle against the odds, to really be in the game and win."
"But you have so much money already—what was it about today? I mean, isn't another two million just a drop in the bucket?"
"Yeah, I have so much money that it makes money without me doing that much. But today I really worked—I took a big risk, and it paid off. It was exhilarating."
"You risking two million dollars is like me betting a quarter and winning five dollars. Wow! I mean, I'm just curious: you already have so much—why do you keep working to make more? How much money do you really need?"
"What kind of ridiculous question is that?"
"I'm just asking. When do you have enough?"
"Enough?"
"When do you stop and say, 'I have enough money to really enjoy my life and help the people that I care about'?"
"Have enough? That's a ridiculous concept. There's no such thing as enough."
"But you can't possibly spend it all in your lifetime."

7. When Is Enough Money Enough?

> "Making money is a competition. Competition is fun."
> "So you're just using moneymaking to make yourself feel good?"
> "What's wrong with feeling good?"
> "Nothing, but what about not just feeling good, but doing good?"
> "I do plenty of good."
> "Yeah, in your spare time, but money only has real value when it does real things."
> "What do you consider real things?"
> "Putting books into readers' hands, desks into schools, computers into homes, gardens in cities, art on walls. Money is energy; how much better could you feel using your fortune to do more of those things than making bets all day?"
> "Those ducks are pretty happy that I'm betting all day."

For the most part, I was grateful to have my job teaching the Klein family, getting both cash and satisfaction from making them better tennis players. As my employer with his own tennis court, Mr. Klein (not his real name) had a *lot* of money—and still does. As of this writing, *Forbes* puts his total net worth at $1.05 billion. At that time I didn't have much money (my total net worth would have been less than what Klein made in an hour), and I was very curious to understand what goes through the mind of a billionaire. When we talked about money and politics, I wasn't a threat to him, so he felt like he could speak to me candidly and we could even tease each other a bit.

I consider myself a "human capitalist," which is my term for anybody that believes making money is a noble and honorable ambition. Financial security is an integral part of a happy and balanced life, and making as much money as you can is beautiful as long as you follow the first rule of human capitalism: the top priority is the welfare of the planet and the human rights of workers. After that, make as much profit as you want. Profits are wonderful, but not at the expense of destroying the planet or causing workers to struggle for survival. This seems pretty basic when your heart and mind are working together.

But Mr. Klein claimed that making more and more money made him happy. I'm pretty happy when I feel like I've got enough shekels to play music and still pay my bills. In both cases, money is an essential part of the happiness experience. Yet there's a very fundamental difference.

So while we might think we know what happiness is, do we know what money is? Why is there a debate about money and evil? Is money the root of all evil? Or as Oscar Wilde wondered, is the *lack* of money the root of all evil?

Money isn't real.

OK, I know what you're thinking. *If money isn't real, try living without it.*

But by *real*, I mean that the paper or the coins or the Bitcoin or the gold has no use besides being a placeholder for. . . . Stick a pin in that idea; we'll be right back.

If money were real, is it as real as a hammer? Nah. They are both "placeholders" in our minds, but a hammer holds a definite place defined by use, while money holds an indefinite place defined by a mix of social norms, personal judgement, luck, and governmental and private policies. Those forces often are unseen and beyond the control of a single person—and so a dollar has no intrinsic value; its value is an agreement: no one person controls it. But a single person *can* control a hammer. The hammer is real. Money? Not so much. A hammer is that "thing that hits nails," and that's what makes a hammer real. It doesn't matter what the

7. When Is Enough Money Enough?

Chinese monetary policy was yesterday, that hammer will work regardless of market forces. Your dollar, on the other hand, will do different things on different days with different people.

And what if you convert your dollar to Venezuelan *bolivars*? The relative value of the bolivar—the currency for an entire nation—in 2018 inflated at 12,874.6 percent. If you had twelve thousand bolivars on January 1st, it was worth one bolivar on December 31st. Inflation has happened at scary rates in the USA, but never twelve thousand to one. But it happened when Hitler rose to power in Germany, when it took a wheelbarrow full of deutschmarks to purchase a single turnip.

So as a concept, money holds a place in our minds as something that's unreal, but very useful and necessary—and that thing is *power*. Not just the amount of money you have, but—and here's the point I was making with Mr. Klein—the way you use it determines your real identity in the world. The money isn't real, but like the hammer for a carpenter, it's how you use it.

Money *is* an amazing tool—you do need a hammer to pound nails—and we do need to earn money (i.e., have a certain amount of power) to pay our expenses in daily life. We use money to know the value of both our labor and our property.

Rather than me taking my hammer to the grocery in exchange for food, I use my hammer, and my time, to do labor. People think it's worth a slice of power, so I get dollars for my effort (which people makes a big difference because, remember, it's negotiation, not truth. When you buy that old desk at a garage sale for fifty dollars because that's all the person thinks it's worth and then negotiate to sell it to some antiques dealer in Palm Beach for thirty-five hundred dollars, what's the truth?)

The money itself has no real value; it's just a placeholder for power. I gave of my power to teach, and I received the power to pay my rent, play music, and do a bit better than just survive. I also got a degree of happiness from doing these things without constantly worrying about making more and more money. Maybe I didn't have a giant 401K, but I had a new Steve Gadd snare drum that sounded amazing, so I was content and creative.

Mr. Klein, however, didn't see things the same way. He wanted the power, but only for the sake of having power. He's very much like Croesus: a king in Greek mythology who was as rich as a man could be, and who got his wealth by doing anything and everything to get money—but still he felt uncomfortable in his skin. He even asked a sage why he wasn't happy. Let's look at that idea for a moment. Why wasn't he happy?

It gets back to the way money and evil are dancing in the same mosh pit. The evil comes from not understanding that money is only a placeholder, and where the evil slips in, the happiness slips out.

If power alone is my reason for getting money, then money has no real meaning for me except that I'm more powerful than you. At that point, any means of getting money is OK because it's all about me being stronger than you. There is no other value in the transaction. Getting more money by any means necessary is the crucial point in this worldview. Isn't that capitalism in a nutshell? (OK, we'll save "capitalism" for another question.)

But if that capitalist virtue reflected reality—if it were a humanly healthy way to be—then Croesus would be the happiest guy around. And Mr. Klein would feel no difference between the emotional connection of playing with his children or scoring a couple million in a day (when he already has a billion and change).

In terms of basic psychology, as Abraham Maslow noticed, you've got to have some money, enough to survive, before you can relax enough to feel happy. Until you feel you have enough

7. When Is Enough Money Enough?

"power" to ensure your survival, your mind is a slave to worry. But once you have enough money to survive, you are free to feel happy—in whatever way you can.

At that point, it's all about how you use your money, not just getting money.

How much money do you need to feel secure? That's the point at which money buys happiness. But this is where a healthy sense of perspective needs to be applied. If you have thirty million dollars and feel like it's not enough, you have completely lost touch with pretty much the entire human race. OK, not true—you and the other thirty-six million millionaires in the world (there are currently eleven million in the US) who make up half a percent of the world's population can all get out your baby violins and lament about how insecure you feel being at the tippy top of the world's financial mountain. "If we just had a hundred million, then we could relax."

When we lose sight of the fact that money is a placeholder for energy, an exchange of value with the community and the world, it becomes a tool of the ego used to measure an illusion of self-worth based on how many gold pieces we have.

So if all you want is "more money" and you don't make a connection between how you make it, how you hold it, and how you spend it, you're missing the way that money connects to happiness. The tragedy is that many people think that "more money" is what life is about. But, money's meaning to you is related to how you get it, and then how you use it. It's value for you is related to how much happiness it brings you. How much do you need?

Do Mr. Klein and 2,042 of his fellow billionaires deserve more wealth than the poorest 3.5 billion people combined? That's .0034 percent of human beings controlling half the world's wealth. What do those two thousand-plus people do to deserve so much more money than they can ever spend? Does one human really need a thousand times more than his brother has, much less a million times more? And while we're on the topic of obscene amounts of money, let's address what Olivier Garret of Garret/Gallard research had to say on the state of money in the world today. As of November 2016, private equity firms, banks, and corporations held a mind-boggling *$50 trillion dollars* of cash reserves. It is just a gigantic bank account that might otherwise be in circulation. Instead, it's cash reserves, only a marker of wealth, not invested, not paying salaries or taxes, not building infrastructure. This is how corporations give themselves a safety net. Their purpose is usually defined in a mission statement about their product or service. This massive amount of cash is being withheld from that purpose as a featherbed for executives against hard times.

Meanwhile, workers below the median wage are worrying about day-to-day survival. If just 5 percent of that money—$2.5 trillion dollars—were used for a common good, two-thirds of America's failing infrastructure could be repaired; it could pay for the United Nations Children's Fund for five hundred years. Public college in the USA could be tuition-free for everyone for five years. The cholera vaccine costs three dollars a pop, and there's not enough of it, so we're talking about enough vaccine to inject the entire world for almost one hundred years. Eliminate malaria? That's merely $8.5 billion, or about 2 percent of that 5 percent. Who would miss a nickel on the dollar? But the total amount stays as cash reserves for corporations in what are sometimes overt contradictions to their mission statements.

Oh, and one last point: with the Robotics Revolution, more and more jobs in modernized countries are going away despite the fact that new workers, many college-educated, enter the

7. When Is Enough Money Enough?

workforce every year. In ten years, with self-driving cars and trucks, automated restaurants, voice-activated and automated checkout, and online "efficiencies (Amazon alone has almost obliterated the book selling industry) there will be little demand for millions of today's jobs. What will these people do? Our Gross Domestic Product will continue to rise faster and faster with automation, but what about our Gross Domestic Happiness?

Is there an actual amount of money that represents "security" in Maslow's paradigm? In the United States in 2015, Princeton University researchers estimated that on average, seventy-five thousand dollars was essential for a family of four. Below that number, the decreasing income meant "decreasing happiness and increasing sadness and stress"; however, once the "basic security level" was met, getting more money didn't mean more happiness, satisfaction, or emotional security. It seems that seventy-five thousand a year for a family of four can buy you happiness to the extent that you don't have to constantly worry about surviving. But once you're making over seventy-five thousand, having $100 million dollars isn't going to make you a whole lot happier. Why not? Because after you provide for survival, how you spend money depends on those other variables: how you spend it, how you contribute to others, how you play with others after you're done earning the dollars.

If there's a relationship between money and happiness, let's look at happiness. Where are the happiest people in the world? According to Alex Horton for the *Washington Post*, in the 2018 *World Happiness Report*'s annual ranking of more than 150 countries, Finland is No. 1, edging out Norway, the 2017 *World Happiness Report* champion. Denmark was third, followed by Iceland and Switzerland. For the second consecutive year, the United States has taken a tumble, at eighteenth, down four spots from a year ago—and America's worst showing since the annual report was introduced in 2012. The United States has never cracked the top ten.

In most significant societal ways, we are basically identical. So what is the critical difference that makes at least ten—and in 2018, almost twenty—countries happier than Americans? The US and the top ten are all technologically advanced countries; we have competitive corporations supporting our economies; we are constitutional democracies; we are rich in intellectual infrastructure and educational institutions. In almost every way, we're similar.

However, there's one dramatic difference: the top ten countries all have vast and effective social safety nets. What's a social safety net? Everyone who lives in a top ten country will be able to survive if he's suddenly unemployed or is injured or has a rare disease; they have free healthcare and, in most of them, free education at every level. They place a higher value on safety and education than the US does.

They pay their teachers a much higher relative wage. They also pay higher taxes, but when surveyed, they see the logical fairness of paying those higher taxes to receive in return free healthcare and education. The higher taxes also result in safer streets, state-of-the-art infrastructure and public transportation, and an excellent workforce. Oh, and they spend proportionately less on their militaries. While some of them allow firearm ownership, it's strictly licensed, and certain kinds of weapons are restricted.

In terms of happiness, are we making an error in relentlessly seeking higher worker productivity and GDP? Are we wrong to make superstars out of the super-wealthy and invest our national identity in a military that costs more than the next eight militarized nations combined?

Not only do the top ten happiest countries have effective social safety nets, they work fewer days, have long vacations and

7. When Is Enough Money Enough?

long maternity leaves, and emphasize social cooperation over status and competition.

When you choose to put happiness in monetary terms, you're choosing fear-based thinking over love-based thinking. Fear-based thinking tells you there's never enough money and, like Mr. Klein, you need to keep fighting for more and more. In the circle of love, there's a sense of sharing and contribution; if everyone respects everyone else enough to contribute to a basic level of humane survival for all, that's the basis for shared happiness and a sense of gratitude.

Love—and freedom—come from contribution. Fear is never having enough.

Sweat This Out

Given what you now know about happiness and money, figure out what your money number might be. How much would you need to have safely in the bank so you won't need to worry about surviving in reasonable comfort—not with a Bentley and a butler, but with a car and groceries.

At the top of a page in your notebook, write your number.

Now, imagine that you've acquired that number: how will you spend your life? You never have to sweat another dollar. You have enough to survive without Fear. Now what?

Eventually, you'll get bored with surfing, sipping, and smoking in some tropical paradise.

To have joy beyond the vague pleasures of being entertained requires challenges beyond a permanent vacation. How will you choose to spend your time—what hobby, job, organizational support, or sport will you pursue? What would you do if you didn't need an income to live on?

The question here is: Who do you want to play with?

It's like kindergarten, except you're grown up now, with all your talents, beliefs, energy, and intelligence. Who are the interesting kids to hang with? What are you curious about? What are you good at?

Take a few minutes to make some lists of possibilities. What job or duty or cause would make you feel valuable, would make your time most interesting? Write down all the ideas you get.

Now you've written down two key thoughts:

an amount of money that's your personal safety net to ensure your survival

some possibilities for how you'd feel connected to the world in an interesting, challenging way that would make you happy

Take that piece of paper and put it next to your cash and credit cards. Every so often take it out and remember to ask, "How much money do I have? Have I hit my number? Have I surpassed my number?"

Love or Fear. Money is the connection.

8. DO YOU HAVE A CONSISTENT MORAL CODE?

After graduating college in my mid-twenties, I got my real estate license and tried my hand at selling properties in the suburbs. It only lasted a short time. One Sunday I was at my desk in a real estate office, which was next to Jen's desk. She'd taken the real estate course with me, so we'd known each other a few months at this point. She had just come from church. She went every Sunday.

I had to ask her if she'd heard what I heard. "Did you hear what Betty Sue just told her client?"

"Betty Sue? No . . . what?"

"She just said that house on Old Pines had a $325,000 offer."

"Yeah, so?"

"So that's complete BS. I heard Terry say right in front of Mr. Jacobs that she had an offer for $310K on that house. She's inflating the price to the other buyer by fifteen grand."

"Gregg, so what? Who knows if that's true, and really it's none of your business."

"Jennifer, what are you talking about? That's the same as stealing."

"Gregg, we're here to sell real estate and make money. We're not the moral police. Betty Sue can say whatever she wants."

"That's not what it says on my real estate license. It says

something about 'honest representation . . .' I don't remember a clause for boldfaced lying."

"That's a little dramatic, don't you think?"

"A little dramatic? What would be a lotta dramatic? Selling a home that doesn't exist?"

"Gregg, you're taking this a little too seriously. It's not that big a deal. Relax. You need to focus on getting your own listings."

"So, a couple grand here or there, a few made-up numbers—that's OK?"

"Gregg, they call it 'real estate,' but it's actually 'unreal estate.' Get over it."

"I must be in the wrong business."

Later that same day, as I thought about Jen and her church, I wondered—would she help herself to that fat twenty-dollar bill on top when the collection plate came by? It seemed like pretty much the same thing to me. I never bothered to ask her about that possibility because obviously she'd be insulted and angry: How could I even think such a thing? But it seems completely logical that if you make stealing OK in one place, you could make it OK in another place. That's not how people see moral choices, though; money at work means something different from money in church. We are very circumstantial in our morals. We apply different codes to different people, places, and value systems—money, property, time. However, they are all, in some ways, connected. "Time is money" is a truth when we get paid for time on the job. What about the person who is always fifteen minutes late? Is that person stealing from their fellow workers who are on time? Is that person stealing from his or her employer?

When I was in negotiations with a music agent at one point in my career, I watched him work out a deal for some really

8. Do You Have a Consistent Moral Code?

offensive—to me anyway—gangsta rap that was misogynistic, violent, homophobic . . . creative rhymes about hating and bragging. I knew that this guy had kids, and he told me in an aside that'd he'd never let his kids listen to these "artists" that were making him a big pile of money with their hateful views.

It seems to me that "hypocrisy" has lost its sting as well as a stigma in the world today. Money can shift our moral compass.

The pursuit of money certainly is one of the primary "looseners" of our moral compass. The pursuit of power is another realm where morality applies. Before 2016, certain American religious organizations were constantly outraged by any personal failings of politicians who transgressed sexually or were discovered telling untruths. Yet after the election of a serial philanderer who has cheated on all of his three wives and is famous for making up his own "facts" on the spur of the moment, these "religionists" (who have quite literally damned other politicians for lesser transgressions) now insist that these are just "human failings" and say they are compelled by their beliefs to forgive and "understand" these "moral shortcomings."

Personally, I believe in forgiveness. But it needs to be a consistent value. Both monotheistic religions and democratic governments share a central belief that treating your neighbor as yourself—holding both to the same standards, privileges, and expectations—is a moral basis for understanding and trust, and a solid foundation for a healthy society. Treating your neighbor as yourself is a good starting point for constructing a moral compass; it's basically following the "Golden Rule": Do unto others as you would have them do unto you. It seems simple enough: treat people the way you want to be treated.

When I meet businessmen with factories overseas that pay people less than a dollar an hour to work eight, ten, sometimes twelve hours a day in less than ideal working conditions, I've often asked them, "Would you work for eighty-five cents an hour in this factory?" They typically reply, "It's different for them." What's different? They're working for almost nothing in difficult and often really unpleasant conditions. They're just as human as you are. How does that coincide with treating people the way you want to be treated? It sounds to me as though they're following the other Golden Rule: He who has the gold makes the rules. Or as the United States Supreme Court likes to call it, the Citizens United decision: corporations can give as much money as they like to political candidates to influence legislation they like. How is that moral?

Morality by definition is simply the concept of right and wrong in our actions and how we treat others; it's how we strive to abide by those beliefs. When I look around at the world, though, it often seems that the weight of gold in someone's pocket has a very persuasive effect on their morality.

How does hypocrisy fit into the question of a moral compass? It turns out that hypocrisy is a really good test of the integrity of your moral compass. If every human being is your neighbor as defined by the Golden Rule, then *everyone* is entitled to your respect, support, and love. But if you are selective in who you see as your neighbor and are loving only to those who profit you in some way that would be an immoral compass.

Jen went to church and professed in her prayers that she would love her neighbor as herself. And while she probably didn't abscond with twenty bucks from the collection plate, a few hours later she condoned Betty Sue's lying to try to get a higher commission on an extra fifteen grand. Stealing from the collection plate and lying about the price both represent ill-gotten gains, and they both are hypocrisies in terms of the Golden Rule. Jen is

8. Do You Have a Consistent Moral Code?

treating her fellow parishioners as her neighbors, not as business relationships. So her fellow parishioners are in the Circle of Love (neighbors), but the real estate clients live in the Sphere of Fear where it's all about profit. Not neighbors, but suckers. Once again, it's very important to think about consistency. Consider how much the Circle of Love opens when there's a consistent moral compass, while the Sphere of Fear makes it easy to have one morality in one place and time, and another in different circumstances.

How about a little thought experiment?

When you pass what appears to be a homeless person on the sidewalk, with his clothes in tatters and his stench reaching you from three feet away, how do you respond? Do you judge his character, determining that his weakness, sexuality, or stupidity have landed him in his current condition? Perhaps you think it would be better if people like him were kept out of sight—maybe in camps or on an island.

Or do you carefully step around him and walk away, feeling sorry for him, but grateful that you've avoided the bad luck or bad home environment that has resulted in this impoverished and unwashed condition?

Or perhaps you offer to help him out with a little money, or food, or a kind word. This is your neighbor, a fellow citizen. As one Christian theologian put it: "There but for the grace of God go I."

Sweat This Out

Get out your notebook and consider three possible moral criteria as separate areas of your life: self-interest, fairness/equality, and honesty. Now make the following headers for these categories:

1. Family and/or relationships
2. Work
3. Money

Think about three events in the past week that left you with some kind of emotional charge. Which of the criteria caused the charge, good or bad? And why?

9. DO YOU HAVE ONE SECRET FEAR THAT IS YOUR CONSTANT COMPANION?

My friend Ben and I were at a sidewalk table having some beers at his favorite pub in Miami. We were watching all the hipsters and tourists doing their evening Miami so-cool struts, and we'd been talking about getting older. Suddenly Ben got this wicked smile on his face.

"What really scares you, Gregg? What are you most afraid of?"
"Most afraid? You mean like nuclear war or economic collapse?"
"Nah. That scares everybody. You personally—what's the fear that's always in the back of your mind—that defines you in some way?"
I had to think for a moment, but then it was clear: "I guess the idea of never falling in love again."
Laughing, Ben said, "You sound like a fifteen-year-old girl. Or maybe a Burt Bacharach song..." He did an imitation of Dionne Warwick, "I'm never gonna fall in love again! Whoa, man. Chee-zeee!"
"No, man, I'm serious. One of the peak experiences of my entire life was true love. I know it can happen again, but I feel real fear that it won't. But I look for it every day."

"What if that train has left the station? What if we're genetically programmed to feel 'true love' at a certain age, and after that, any 'soulmate' we find is at a lower temperature, longer cook time, and needs more of our conscious attention?"

"Oh, man. Why are you pissing in my beer? I don't want to believe that."

"OK, believe what you want, but honestly, you know what it sounds like to me?"

"I know you're going to tell me anyway..."

"I think you're afraid of getting old and being alone. "

"Who're you calling old?"

"That's why you have this young-ass fantasy about 'true love.' My point is, you do all this New Age love stuff; you meditate and pray. You're humble and grateful and all, and you say it works for you. But deep down, you've got this fear/fantasy that runs you. You 'look for it every day.' You're just like so many other people. Everyone has a fear/fantasy that they don't want to examine too closely. This idea that you're going to have the young true love experience again—I think that kind of energized love-beam is just for young people who aren't really formed yet."

"Yes, OK. I can see that in my fear, I'm wishing I'm never going to get old and I imagine I'll have a companion who'll help me feel young."

"Forever young? Nice idea. Bad reality adjustment."

"You've got a point. But I'm trying to face this uncomfortable feeling, and it's a damned uncomfortable part of me."

"Can you face it?"

"Yeah. I can admit that a part of me is yearning for the energy of true love, and yes, the last time I felt it was when I was much younger, and yes, I'm more formed as a person now—but I still believe I can feel that way. At the same time, I don't have any

9. Do You Have One Secret Fear That Is Your Constant Companion?

expectation of how it's supposed to be. I know that I'm older and a little slower and the rest of that biology stuff, but I still believe in love in whatever form it comes in. Real love is real love whether you're fifteen, thirty, sixty, or ninety. And I'm going to keep believing in it until I either find it or die."

So, for you—maybe your secret fear is different from my now not-so-secret fear:

maybe you're afraid you'll fail in business;

that your spouse will leave you;

that your children will die before you;

that you'll always hate your job;

that you'll always be in debt;

that you'll always feel lonely and left out;

that your children will hate you;

that you'll never finally get sober;

Etc., etc., etc.

Most of us don't want to think about our fears. But if you're aware of that one secret fear, can you see that it is always in the back of your head, a constant hum of anxiety, like a dentist's drill in the next room?

If you can locate that one special anxiety, your secret fear, you'll have located a super-power. No fear is just one fear; there's a complex of beliefs that give that chief fear its hold on us. Once you put your finger on the key, you can use attention to unpack the jumble of memories and beliefs and see how real or unreal they are.

Admitting these intimate fears—observing how they control you—is the first step to getting control of them.

Next, who can you talk to? You want to choose someone you trust who will be able to step back from a relationship with you and be dispassionate and objective: a close friend or a professional, a clergyman, mentor, or sponsor in a program. You can reach out to them and suggest a dialogue with you in which they agree to just listen, not judge, and especially *not give advice*. The point of this conversation is to assist you in acknowledging your fear.

A word of warning: beware of doing this step with family and relationship partners. Often our most intimate and long-lasting relationships are built on agreeing with us that our fears are justified. We train our intimates to give us feedback that feeds the fear. In the initial stages of sharing your feelings about your fear, it's probably best to find someone who has an interest in you, but not a deep or long-standing emotional attachment to you. You want them to have some emotional objectivity. You won't scare them by telling them the truth. This action is an important step in loving yourself.

Once you've seen and acknowledged your fears, the next step is finding the love to conquer them. That sounds schmaltzy, but it's not lovey-dovey love—"Oh, I kiss myself, and it's going to be all right!" No, this is honest, tough love.

Being honest with yourself is the ultimate in self-love. Choosing to honestly unpack your fears will expand your consciousness so you can see that what you had been accepting as "natural" isn't natural at all; self-love comes from seeing who you really are, and in some way accepting it enough to share it with whomever you're talking to (which is why they must agree not to judge.) You don't need to fix the fear; you don't need to change your life—you just want to take a look at what you're afraid of. Tell that story; if there's a memory or some recent event associated with the fear, what was it?

9. Do You Have One Secret Fear That Is Your Constant Companion?

One thing to talk about is how you present yourself. Is it possible that you are doing things in such a way that you are actually asking to have your fear justified? Notice how your expectations and behaviors may seem to lead you to difficulties. That's called projection.

We *project* our fear and people respond to the fear, but it's all very unconscious. Let's say you have a date with a person you're attracted to. If you're afraid you'll be rejected, you may find yourself pointing out your own shortcomings—maybe you *think* you're "being honest," but your "honesty" is really a choice that will create rejection by showing your less-attractive self. If you didn't have the secret fear of rejection, you could talk about the wealth of attractive qualities—your passions and strengths—that are also honest representations *and* would make you look attractive. Instead, you project your fear and make it easy to get rejected. By choosing to show your shortcomings, you're giving the other person a reason not to ask you for a second date. Why do that? Some of those shortcomings may never even show up.

When you don't get the second date, you've proven your fear to yourself—"It's true! I'm unlovable and worthless!"—and that's called a "self-fulfilling prophecy." Your projected fear was the prophet of your own disappointment. You did it!

It's easy to be attached to our fears and think they are "real."

I recently had a conversation with my dentist's assistant. She's always been a little anxious when we've talked, but this time she was telling me how she was going to visit family out west but was petrified of flying and didn't know what to do. I guess I could've said, "Don't worry, your plane won't crash," but all she would have heard was "plane crash!" (I did pause to reflect on how she'd chosen to work in a dental office, a place where many people are afraid and anxious about pain, needles, teeth falling out—it's not a chill environment, so she'd found a way to connect with anxiety every day in her working life.) Instead I said, "I have an idea—why don't you try using virtual reality to experience what flying is like while still safely on the ground?" With VR, she would know she was safe, and she could then transfer that experience so she'd have the feelings of *both* flying and being safe before she got on the plane.

She didn't want to try it, though. In a way, she didn't want to be fully conscious of her fear. I had to think that maybe she kind of wanted to hang on to her fear. It was part of her belief system. Habits are very comfortable . . . even the uncomfortable ones.

You probably know someone who constantly complains about life. They can't get a break. Certain kinds of situations—job, romance, money, family—just "never work out" for them. If it happens over and over again, there's a good chance that this is their projection. Their fear-created prophecy is being fulfilled.

By discussing your fear with someone else, you'll see it more fully. And you'll possibly even diffuse the self-fulling prophecy, which will help you to create new, more loving experiences. When you're having this discussion, tell them about your thoughts and behaviors, anything you do that in some way reflects this fear. Do you fantasize that your lover will leave you or do you plan to be together forever? Do you focus on your children's success, or do you fixate on peanut allergies and bus crashes? Do you present your strengths with a smile or your doubts with a moan? In your social interactions, other people will feel your fear and behave as if it were true. This is an automatic function in people; they're not being mean, just agreeable. Whatever fear you project, others will pick up on it and tend to agree with it.

Life is challenging for everyone, and we all struggle with fears. While some people's fears are more debilitating and demand

9. Do You Have One Secret Fear That Is Your Constant Companion?

greater immediate attention than others, most of us struggle with some fear that haunts us. Perhaps the fully enlightened yogis and saints are fear-free, but the rest of us need to find the courage and strength to look our fear square in the face.

Facing our fears is hard. It is uncomfortable, and it can upset our routines, even the way we show ourselves to friends and family. But once we identify a specific, dominating fear in our mind—the moment the dominating character crystallizes and we admit the power the fear has over us—at that moment we start to take our power back from the fear. Just recognizing the fear won't be enough to erase it. You've spent a lifetime—or a chunk of a lifetime—with this habit of fearfulness. It has deep hooks in your beliefs about yourself. You've got to find the courage to look at it and eventually talk about it. It's actually that simple—sorry. Yeah, I know there are a million reasons you can't talk about it, but if you're going to overcome this menacing, sneaky, controlling fear, you've got to find a way to bring it into the light.

As Woody Allen once said, "Eighty percent of life is showing up." There you have it. You control who shows up: your fearful self or the self you love.

Sweat This Out

If you haven't found a nonjudgmental friend to share with yet, get your pen out. You're going to write down all your possible fears. Find "the one," even if it seems a little wacky. This is what you can talk about—and remember, you don't need the answer before you talk.

10. HOW DO YOU KNOW WHAT YOU KNOW?

What is the difference between what you think and what you know? Many of us think what we know is The Truth.

> Before his tennis lessons, Mr. Klein would sometimes take me for a long ride in his golf cart over the rolling hills of his estate. He liked to share the beauty of the luxurious flora and fauna with a young man he could talk to—and who probably never would have a personal golf cart and thirty acres of manicured gardens. We both enjoyed the cart rides as an opportunity to discuss issues because we were enthusiastic arguers with completely different worldviews. But because we liked each other so much, we could disagree and then hop out of the cart and have a really good tennis lesson.
>
> We were on a path skirting the pond, and I'd said something that got him going. "We need to have news media, and they need to have sponsors. That's how it works, Gregg. Why are you so against corporate media?"
>
> "I'm not necessarily against corporate media; I'm just suspicious if I hear the same talking points repeated over and over again."
>
> "So you're claiming they're biased and out to deceive?"
>
> "Well, Mr. K, yes, they're biased. But they're inside the box created by their corporate owners, so they can't see their biases."

"The news is the news. Things happen, and the media reports them."

"'Things happen?' If things happen that threaten wealthy people, yeah. If things happen to upset the traditions of government, well, they'll probably get reported too. Why? Because the news media is owned by rich white men (and a few women) who are hooked into the government and who must make those things—whiteness, wealth, and government—into 'important' and entertaining ideas."

"So what's your point? What do you think the news should be about?"

"My point is that the news should cover 'real events' from multiple perspectives, whether it's poor Malaysians working as slaves for our Saudi allies or the .01 percent of 1 percent who control the major news corporations. You have to admit that there is a bias toward the news keeping our attention on wealthy American interests."

"Oh c'mon, Gregg. You sound like some lefty freak."

"I'm not a 'freak'; I'm a realist. I'm all about the deep reality of what's really happening. Let me give you just one example: the Vietnam War."

"Everybody knows Vietnam was a huge mistake..."

"But they didn't until the news stopped reporting what the military claimed was true and went to Vietnam to see what was actually happening. The public saw the photographs and videos coming over the news showing the carnage and suffering that the American war machine—which, by the way, is still fifty cents of every tax dollar you and I pay—was inflicting."

"It's over, Gregg."

"It's over because back then we had more honest and in-depth reporting that showed what was actually happening to

10. How Do You Know What You Know?

poor Asian people fighting a rich colonial power. But now we've been fighting wars in Iraq and Afghanistan, and what kind of video have we seen?"

"We don't really need to see it, Gregg."

"But the point is this: we did see the truth in Vietnam. Our nation saw images of My Lai; we saw what Agent Orange did; we saw napalm used on civilians. But today because of the reaction to the Vietnam coverage, the military prohibits the press from having access to the battlefront. We never see what drone strikes in Afghanistan do or what the firefights in the streets of Fallujah or Baghdad look like, because they know public opinion could turn against the war if we knew the truth. Reporting is kept inside the box, and the military and corporate interests construct that box."

"Sounds like you won't be getting a job at NBC anytime soon," Mr. Klein said as he kicked the cart into gear, and we rode off toward the tennis court.

Mr. Klein would agree that our opinions are based on our "knowledge" of the world. He and I can agree that part of that knowledge comes from information we get from the news media, which then turns into belief systems. Based on what we see and hear, we make evaluations, both moral and ethical, about politicians, people, nations, and our neighbors. Seeing, knowing, and believing are intimately connected. It's worthwhile to wonder: Who controls what I see? How does what I see create what I know?

Might there be a problem when information is mediated by for-profit news corporations? I grew up, like most kids, watching network and local TV news and accepting it as the truth. Journalism is supposed to be unbiased—at least that's what most media outlets claim. When I was young, I had no idea how for-profit news organizations ran; I had no idea how stories were developed. The network news anchors on the evening news—Walter Cronkite, Dan Rather, Ted Koppel—were "the most respected men in the nation." If it appeared on the evening news, I believed it, as did the majority of Americans.

However, when I started college in Purchase, New York, I started listening to WNYC, which is in the NPR (National Public Radio) network. What I heard was completely different from what I heard from Dan Rather. My eyes and ears were opened to longer news stories, more complicated data-based information, and different sides I had never considered before to familiar stories. But maybe more importantly, the news coverage wasn't constantly being interrupted by distracting and obnoxious commercials. I could listen to the news and really get absorbed in it. NPR was "listener-supported," not corporate-owned. As "national radio," they did get a slice of their operating budget from Washington, and they did get a little bigger slice from corporate contributions, but the bulk of their budget was supplied by individual contributors from all over the political spectrum, and that was why their coverage sounded so different. Even self-proclaimed "impartial" for-profit news organizations had to portray the news in such a way as to not offend their advertisers. In some news organizations, there was a "wall" between the news and the advertising departments; they weren't supposed to affect each other or even know about each other's doings. But the fact that advertisers have an interest in how the news is portrayed exerts a pressure on the best intentions of any for-profit media news organization. Listening to NPR, I started to doubt the truth of what I heard on for-profit news stations.

Today many people have developed a distrust of the for-profit

10. How Do You Know What You Know?

news industry. In part this is because corporate interests have become more obvious in the past twenty years. This is where the concept of fake news comes from. There is a corporate bias in what gets reported.

The question of environmental degradation is a case in point. For years, for-profit news media, supported by polluting oil companies, have not reported the full extent of the oncoming climate change. Other media, NPR in particular, have reported how many climate scientists are predicting severe worldwide weather disruptions as the result of man-made pollution. If 98 percent of non-corporate scientists agree global warming is real, well, those are fact-driven people. If the oil companies or their paid-for representatives tell you there's no such thing as global warming, what do you think they have in mind: facts or profits?

The current furor about "fake news" is the result of one man's (the 45th president of the United States') intense insecurity and complete and utter intolerance for anyone that disagrees with his agenda. Depending on what you think you already know or what side of the political fence you're on, you can choose which news you want to believe. Anything else is fake news. Corporate news has become a political tool that feeds into the basic psychology of confirmation bias, which I will talk about shortly.

What I'm going to say next is a strongly held belief of mine that you may not agree with. But bear with me; I want to show how what I believe is based on what I see.

In recent history, a good example of the for-profit media bias was in the run-up to the American invasion of Iraq. Although Iraq had nothing to do with the tragedy of 9/11, somehow the coverage was conflating Saddam Hussein and Iraq with that attack, and there were persistent rumors about Saddam's relationship to Al-Qaeda and "weapons of mass destruction."

27 QUESTIONS TO MAKE YOU SWEAT

All the major networks started putting huge American-flag backdrops on their evening news coverage, and some even had a print header, "The March to War." But what was the reason? My beloved NPR managed a degree of skepticism, yet still did not invalidate claims of WMDs—although there had been some evidence Saddam destroyed the ones he had—nor did they invalidate the connection of Iraq with Al-Qaeda, despite the fact that there was solid reporting on how Saddam hated and distrusted Bin Laden, and vice versa.

How did I know this? Because I had picked up on another radio station at this time, Pacifica, thinking it sounded like NPR; there were reasonable voices doing in-depth stories, relaying facts, and sourcing information from knowledgeable sources. But it didn't take long for me to realize that what they were saying was, for the most part, almost the exact opposite of what I heard on the major networks, and even a far cry from NPR's sanitary middle-of-the-road reporting. Pacifica was overtly anti-war. They weren't middle-of-anything. They saw corrupt corporate and news interests as railroading the American people into acquiescing and accepting what would be a disaster in Iraq (the government deciding to make war, not the media). I had tuned in to a whole different perspective on events, a whole new world. One of the six stations in the Pacifica Network, New York's WBAI, was (and still is) entirely listener-supported—no corporations, no think tanks, no government bucks. WBAI reporters were unafraid to out the lies told about WMDs and Al-Qaeda; they exposed the clear connections between American mega-corporations supplying the military with the tools and supplies to destroy and rebuild infrastructure and the news organizations eager to attract more listeners by having an exciting war to report on. They gave multiple history lessons on the similarity to the war in Vietnam and the

10. How Do You Know What You Know?

cycle of government disinformation and corporate pressures that led to that disastrous and expensive adventure in hell.

The WBAI coverage was completely different from anything I was hearing anywhere in the news media, but what accounted for the difference? Because Pacifica had no corporate or government contributors, they were free to question that corporate and government point of view at every turn. Pacifica contributors were donating so they could hear their news from the points of view of working people, poor people, and simply curious people; they valued opinions that weren't popped out of corporate-funded think tanks or political party central committees. They wanted to hear independent thinkers like Noam Chomsky, Chris Hedges, and Cornel West, who saw that there was a controlling set of interests shared by both left- and right-wing news media, a point of view that was mostly a class interest of wealthy white men.

That viewpoint was "naturalized" by all the major news media. However decent and balanced NPR tries to be, any attempt to find the "center" of the news will be corrupted by those who hold power: the story is modified by its relationship to where the money is. NPR's perspective has always been slanted through the intellectual and economic elite from the coasts, and their ethos of giving everyone equal coverage means that they are reluctant to call out think tanks like the Heritage Foundation and The Cato Institute—which are no more than privately funded propaganda machines, despite being staffed with PhDs.

As any Pacifica listener will tell you, most think tanks are not impartial information-gathering institutions, but instead are funded by and in the interests of special-interest groups. Yes, there are some left-leaning think tanks out there, but more than half of them are funded by super-rich, far-right-wing conservatives such as the Koch Brothers and the Mercer and DeVos families.

27 QUESTIONS TO MAKE YOU SWEAT

Nevertheless, Pacifica invites their representatives to offer opinions next to liberals who don't have huge sugar daddies giving them expense accounts and who aren't creating "data" to fit corporate profit agendas. Pacifica is always careful to call out where the money for any opinion or database comes from. Also, their coverage names names when it comes to polluters, violators, fraudsters, and other criminals from the corporate or government classes.

    Let's get back to the question of what we know and how we know it. When I was growing up, I only knew what the network news showed me. What I was being shown was filtered through the for-profit lens of corporate news. Much of it might have been factual, but it was limited and focused by rich, white men. When I learned about NPR, it was a revelation, because NPR brought other colors and classes into the discussion. Yet NPR was still drawing support from powerful institutions—the same educational pool and socioeconomic would-be rulers. They were drawing from people who had gotten power in traditional ways, perhaps not as lily-white or masculine, but they all talked similar talk and shared many of the same assumptions about the world. Even if their people came from different backgrounds, different classes, and different cultures, they'd been trained in the same institutions, so over time they'd been shown the same things, read the same books, and therefore all had the same way of "knowing" the world. They were unaware of how their point of view was shaped by the money and institutions that supported the "infotainment" they provided. An example is NPR's point-counterpoint format, where they present nonprofit public servants and university professors debating with the well-paid representatives of political think tanks. This is a false equivalency because the professors aren't getting paid to come up with a certain outcome; they're doing research and coming up with

10. How Do You Know What You Know?

whatever the facts bear out. The think tank talking heads are pushing an agenda and pretending that it comes from "research," when in fact they're being paid large sums of money to argue for the viewpoint of their wealthy benefactors, whether individuals or corporations. Compared to network news, it is more objective, but the filter of class and money still distorts their knowledge—which is clear if your point of view is from outside Washington, D.C., and the corporate capitalism system.

The viewpoint of people trying to make money and the viewpoint of people trying to make peace are at times diametrically opposed. Corporations exist to sell stuff, and the stuff they sell needs to seem necessary. Whether it's a war in the Middle East or state-of-the-art underwear, a political candidate or a new car, somewhere in the sales pitch is an appeal to fear. When corporations navigate the boat many of us find ourselves in, they set us at each other's throats, while they have exclusive rights to the lifeboats. Pacifica came from a different point of view: that we're all in the same boat and we need to get along with each other and help each other when necessary. If you're trying to make money, you will traffic in fear. Fear sold the Iraq war because fear sells. It appeals to our most animal like nature and always frames things in terms of competitions. It's very hard to drill down on what you think you know and separate fear from reason, yet reason is where authentic love comes from.

Human psychology is the science of how minds work—thinking, memory, genetics, automatic responses, habit and choice. The study of psychology wants to understand how each individual mind is a construct of these factors, and why the actions of these basic components make some individuals happy, healthy, and realistic while others are unhappy, unhealthy, and unrealistic.

Psychology has shown that all human beings are born sharing similar basic capabilities for sensation, emotion, and a specifically human ability for complicated thought. Unless an infant has a DNA abnormality or an infantile disease, once we begin to experience perceptions *in utero*, we all get almost exactly the same equipment for "knowing the world." Even in the womb, we have perceptual systems: we can hear, smell, taste, touch, and feel ourselves within our skin. Once we pop out, our eyes take a while to be able to see, but seeing eventually proves to be our most dominant perception (i.e., most of the brain becomes visually organized). Along with perceptual sensations, every human baby is born with a set of seven basic emotions: happiness, anger, fear, surprise, disgust, sadness, and contempt. Emotions are always responses to *perceptions*. These essential emotions tell us what to "know" by what we feel. They connect perception to an emotion that either feels good or bad, and that's how we begin to form values. They guide our physical responses to get away from bad feelings and go toward good feelings. These cues—which are spontaneous when we're little—help us to first navigate and then organize the world of perception. Later, when we have many memories of perceptions and their associated feelings, we form identities around pursuing what we've learned makes us feel good while avoiding things we've learned to fear, because we don't like bad feelings.

The most miraculous human ability is that, working from perceptions and guided by emotions, our very big brains learn to think in an intricate and organized way. Language is the processing system that big brains use for big ideas. When human babies are exposed to language—when they hear and recognize words spoken by caregivers—their perceptions and emotions engage to make memory associations. Our hearing is designed to perceive the tones and range of the human voice, and in fact, our faces and

10. How Do You Know What You Know?

vocal chords have evolved in the last 100,000 years specifically for speaking. But even before they can actually talk, babies understand when they're spoken to. It's a mystery how the brain does this, and many psychologists believe that the human brain is structured to perceive language before learning to speak, in the same way the hearing and speaking parts of the body have become specialized. And the great key to human thinking is our ability to use words in long combinations to make stories that connect to emotions. Language is the most complex human tool, and when we start to use language, our brains change and become structured by stories. Being able to imagine mental events in the past and future gives us a sense of control, of self, and an awareness of what is possible in the world: this is what we call *consciousness*. *Consciousness* has a wide range of meanings, but for this chapter, it's what psychologists refer to as "awareness of self." We become self-aware of ourselves as expressing wants and thoughts that are different from other people so that our (self) consciousness tells us: "I'm the main character in the story of my life! It started when I was born, and . . . (I don't want to think about the end)."

Our consciousness is organized to imagine life as a story. Any story involves a logical progression of cause and effect, and that chain of one-thing-leading-to-another is what keep us engaged. In a story, we follow what the main character wants as he or she solves a problem or goes for a goal. In the same way, wanting is the driving force in "the story" of our lives. We want to survive, feel happy, have good relationships, and feel that we spend our time in a "meaningful" way. *Meaningful*, of course, means many different things to different people—but the fundamental point is that we tell ourselves the story of what we know in order to get what we want in whatever way each of us believes is most meaningful. The operative word here is believe. Perhaps you believe that getting new jeans will help you score in the sexual arena; perhaps you believe that your mother loved you even though she sexually abused you; perhaps you believe that an MFA from Yale makes you a superior person; perhaps you believe that all you need in life is a loin cloth and a begging bowl.

Beliefs, at the root, are really stories.

Each of us is our own special consciousness, our "me-ness," that's been formed over time from a chain of cause-and-effect relationships between our perceptions and the emotions that comprise these subtle systems (stories) of belief. What we're often not aware of is that those beliefs guide our perceptions: our vision doesn't really see everything in the visual field, but it finds what we want and what we fear. That's what tells us what we "know" about the world.

Consider the notion of "free will" along with "common sense." Many people assume that certain kinds of knowledge should be "common sense." Some people regard it to be "common sense" that everyone born in the United States has the same opportunities as everyone else, because they all have "free will." But let's look at one small aspect of that so-called equal opportunity: how we learn language. A famous study started in 1982 called the Hart-Risley study showed that by the age of three, children from America's wealthiest families have been exposed to *30 million more words* than most children from poor families. Even at age three—before they could read or speak in very complicated ways—the children who had been exposed to more words were more successful with simple cognitive tasks, so they were more comfortable with language-rich relationships and better able to identify a wide range of images. For these wealthy children, their familiarity with language was a pleasant experience; while for the poorer children, less exposure meant that language challenges a little later in life,

10. How Do You Know What You Know?

such as learning to read, were very stressful. The stories of these children's lives had begun taking shape while in the womb, hearing conversations before they could talk—so *before they could even talk*, their opportunities already were limited, and their "free will" had nothing to do with it. But this "common-sense" belief-story that so many people "know" is true is that in America everyone has an equal opportunity for success. *Hmm.*

Let's take a step back and look more deeply at belief-formation.

Yes, our beliefs and knowledge come from emotionally charged experiences we have had as the main character in our own life, but it comes from other places as well. We also learn beliefs from the stories we're told about other characters' lives—whether real or fictional. Stories in media, movies, or books can be so emotionally powerful that they can shape our beliefs with even more strength than events in our own lives. And they work fast! A story well told can deliver emotional experiences in a much more organized way than life itself. In life, we often don't realize what has affected us for months, or even years. But a compelling movie or book can show us a "truth" about life in short order. Our twenty-eighth president (1913–1921), Woodrow Wilson, believed in the power of movies. Wilson was a Virginian from the Old-South mentality, and after viewing the film *Birth of a Nation* at the White House in 1915, he declared: "It is like writing history with lightning. And my only regret is that it is all so terribly true."

Although *Birth of a Nation* was a fantasy representation about the birth of the Klu Klux Klan and in no way represented actual historical events, the movie images of this fantasy of white fear was so stimulating to Wilson that he imagined it was true. And the film had a similar effect on white audiences' beliefs and "knowledge"— so much so that it caused race riots in many large cities.

Almost seventy-five years later, film critics were still so sensitive to the power of fictional movies to spark emotional responses that when Spike Lee's movie *Do the Right Thing* depicted very real contemporary tensions between races and classes of Americans, some of these writers warned of possible riots. Those riots never materialized—but here's a key difference: *Do the Right Thing* was based on undeniable facts, not paranoid fantasies. So instead of riots, the film caused a national debate on race—because it was accurate in the way it showed both black and white points of view. Unlike *Birth of a Nation*, which clearly advised white folks to cut holes in bedsheets and terrorize the neighborhood, *Do the Right Thing* didn't advise the audience what "the right thing to do" might be. It had no easy answers. But the honesty of the story—in which each character was a little wrong and a little right—changed what people thought they "knew."

Every one of us holds our beliefs as true, even to the point of survival, of life and death. But because much of that "knowledge" and consequent beliefs come from stories, this means that our moral sense of the world can depend on what movies we see, what books we read (if we read), where we tune in to the news (if we tune in to the news)—and even what stories we get from advertising, group meetings, Instagrams, and so on. The question is: What stories are we tuning in to?

Therefore, a key to knowing what we know is asking: Where did my knowledge come from? Self-critical thinking is vital; if we don't actively examine our beliefs, we can become subject to unconscious prejudice and possibly manipulation. Unquestioning trust and enthusiasm for our own beliefs is called "confirmation bias." Like Wilson seeing *Birth of a Nation* as "all so terribly true," our inner storyteller is always looking to confirm what we already believe and has difficulty focusing on anything to the contrary. We get great pleasure from confirming our beliefs. We're afraid of

10. How Do You Know What You Know?

having to change them. Even if we think of ourselves as unbiased observers, our ability to see what's in front of us is actually very limited. Our minds filter everything we see, hear, smell, etc., so we look for cues that will confirm what we already "know"—and we "know" that our way of seeing is correct.

And it's not just Wilson "seeing" history in a movie fantasy. Almost everyone has a feeling about people who look different from themselves—those incompetent old people, those lazy millennials, those stupid jocks, those uncoordinated nerds, those crybaby women, those insensitive men . . . you know how it goes. If you have a belief about troublesome old people, you will no doubt find yourself stuck behind an overcautious AARP member in traffic and forget all about the fact that Jimmy Carter or Ronald Reagan were able to achieve so much well after their seventieth birthdays. That's confirmation bias. Perception isn't about "reality"—it's about the version of reality we are emotionally invested in "knowing" to be true.

Today, American politics is divided by two opposing passionate beliefs: one that believes the government is the problem, and another that believes the government can provide solutions. If you believe that "the government is the problem," you will delight in stories about government failures or politicians' fecklessness; you will find a news feed that tells you such stories. If you have the contrary belief that through the government we can find solutions, you will look for progressive stories about how the government problem-solves effectively, and you'll be attracted to politicians who have visions of an engaged democracy.

However, if we think critically, we will see that with blanket statements about the government, neither can be totally true. At least not when there are elections—which make government a changeable social contraption. The truth must be more of a middle position: that government is a complex negotiation between those who are governed and those who govern, and the government is neither always the problem nor always the solution. So, while you may feel emotionally attached to one or the other belief, that bias only makes you easy to manipulate. It's not your rational mind but confirmation bias that makes such reflexive beliefs possible.

But if you think critically, you will be somewhat wary of appeals to your emotions. If you find yourself yelling at the TV, beware! Second, you'll try to find facts and patterns in arguments and outcomes. That's the reason for the question "How do you know what you know?" And that's a reason to look with some suspicion at the "information" you get from any news media source, religious or internet organization, local chamber of commerce, athletic team, political party, etc.—they all create silos of information that really just show their own confirmation biases.

10. How Do You Know What You Know?

Sweat This Out

Pick a problem in the news and research it in three different media landscapes.

First, go to cable news, preferably a station with a strong slant to the left or right, and listen to their version of the story.

Then take a look at your local PBS station or listen to NPR; these are outlets that don't have commercial sponsors, but do have limited corporate funding—what's their version? Is there a difference in emotional tone? In the way the story is told or focused? In the actual facts reported?

Third, find a media outlet that has zero sales pitches for investors, grants-in-aid, religious backers, or their own exclusive line of products (not easy to do!). You can find Pacifica Radio on the internet; they are wholly listener-supported. Listen to their take and then compare and contrast for yourself what the differences are.

For all three, see if you can sense what the appeals are underneath the stories. Can you tell whose interest the "reporting" represents? How much airtime is spent on reporting, and how much on advertising? Can you detect which stories are using fear to draw you in and which have love as their basis? [Broadly understand *fear* as the pretense of "revealing a villain or an enemy," while *love* is a constructive story: reasonable, objective, and maybe even optimistic.]

11. HOW DOES YOUR PERSPECTIVE AID OR HINDER YOU?

Perspective? It's the frame you put on your experience. In the Sphere of Fear, you may hear a complaint like: "The scratch on my iPhone is like totally ugly, but I only have two hundred Instagram followers, so maybe I don't have to replace it today" or "I mean, why am I always in the slowest checkout line? Life is so unfair!"

In the Circle of Love: gratitude, Crazee Gratitude!

> *I was rummaging through the refrigerator in our "new home"—I know there was mayonnaise in here somewhere—when suddenly the tiny kitchen of our two-bedroom house reverberated with my mom's voice.*
>
> *"Your father is crazy. He's drinking all the time; he's lying to me; he's rarely home. I don't know which way is up any more."*
>
> *"Don't worry about it, Mom; it's going to be OK."*
>
> *"What are you talking about, OK? Are you living in the same dream world your father lives in? Open your eyes, Gregg. What part of this reality aren't you seeing?"*
>
> *"Mom, my eyes are open. I see what's going on. It's not the pretty part of the world, but we're doing OK. I know this isn't as nice as the old house, but it's still pretty nice."*
>
> *"Pretty nice? There is no telephone in this house, Gregg.*

There's almost no furniture. We have heat four days out of the week—we are not doing OK."

"Yeah, compared to everyone around here, this isn't flippin' Westchester County, but compared to the rest of the world . . ."

"We don't live in the rest of the world. We live here, and we have almost nothing."

"Mom, you know that's not true. It's rough, I understand, but we're still living in a house—we're not homeless."

"Your father went bankrupt—did you forget that?"

"I think we need to keep some kind of perspective. You know, focus on what's real? What matters? It can make it easier."

"What's the perspective? No money is no money. It doesn't matter where you are."

"But look at where we are, even with almost no money: Lizzie's in college—she's got loans—you and Scott and I have each other and a place to live. Yeah, it's just for now, as long as Dad pays the rent, but we're not on the street. It could be a lot worse. And I feel like it will get better. We have the future ahead of us."

Perspective is the way we "see" the world—we use our sense of perspective with our vision to know how close or far things are—but it works the same way regarding ourselves. We keep perspective when we see the big picture; we lose perspective when we only see our immediate selves.

When I start to lose perspective and start worrying about a problem—like the gig I didn't get or the phone call that still hasn't been returned—well, I have to tell myself to pause. If I take the long view of my life, if I compare my life to others who are walking the earth, missing a phone call isn't a life-changing or life-threatening problem. I think about the refugee camps in Sudan or the slave auctions currently happening in Libya. Those

11. How Does Your Perspective Aid or Hinder You?

are real problems and I'm wasting energy with whatever pity party or frustration fest I'm having for myself. I try to keep in mind the words of Richard Bach: "Perspective, use it or lose it."

To assist my perspective, I remind myself that I'm one of seven billion plus people alive today, and according to the World Bank, over three billion of us live on less than $2.50 a day. That makes it a little harder to get my undies in a knot over one gig: there will be others. I look around and listen, though, and notice angry energy everywhere because of what people think they deserve, which is distracting them from being grateful for what they have. Self-importance gets blown out of proportion with this perspective, so it seems like the grocery store line or a child's bad attitude or a speeding ticket is the end of the world. It's not, but if your*self* is all you see, then it can seem that way. That's when your perspective will hinder you.

When we blow up our self-importance, it prevents us from seeing the future, and it magnifies momentary discomfort like anxiety and anger. That kind of energy actually makes us sick. Fury causes an increase in cortisol, and cortisol causes heart disease. When we start feeling anxious, afraid, angry, despondent, or depressed, those are cues alerting us to be cautious, to find our way around the emotion that is in some way irrational.

When you put things in perspective, you are in the here and now; you see yourself in relation to your wider surroundings, and you stay grounded, seeing all the possibilities. When you lose perspective, your vision is clouded by your immediate fears and all you see is your emotional upset. To reestablish perspective, look for the cause of your emotional upset, see what you can control, and let everything else go. Control is the key; if you have no control, you will get lost in the emotion and lose your power to change anything. The trick is to change what you can and let go of what you can't. My mom couldn't let go of the house we had spent so many good years in, and she also couldn't let go of the idea that my dad could no longer provide for us.

The power of negative emotions is that, in the moment, they dominate our nervous systems: FIGHT-OR-FLIGHT! Yet those emotions are just disguises for fear, which we are designed to get over. We can't live constantly in a state of fight-or-flight without making ourselves physically ill.

Emotions often seem so life-changingly huge, and you feel like you have no choice but to stay wrapped up in pain: when you've lost your job, discover your lover's been loving someone else, or when your 401K has lost its value (as happened to so many people during the crash of '08). Yes, those negative emotions are natural expressions, but *hanging on to them* is a critical loss of realistic perspective. When you hang on to bad feelings, living in them, feeling victimized, none of that will get your life back. Fear is always backward-looking, and power is in the now, in moving forward.

To bring yourself back to the now, ask one simple question: What do I have to FEEL GRATEFUL for? That's where your strength and courage will come from.

> "We lost everything in the flood, but we have each other and our cats, so we're looking for a new house."
>
> "Nadine left me, but I'm healthy and horny, and there are other girls out there."
>
> "I thought I could trust my business partner; damn, well, I'm glad the bastard's gone now."

That's keeping perspective on what matters. If you want to take a long soaky sob in spilled milk, go for it! But if you start to

11. How Does Your Perspective Aid or Hinder You?

get tired of whimpering over what might have been, and you're willing to keep your heart and mind on the future and what's possible, and the powers you have that you're grateful for, now you're moving forward.

In those moments of emotional crisis—like the way my mom was feeling—it's easy to get overwhelmed by our personal fears and forget our universal connections. (We live in a connected universe and we have quantum mechanics to thank for that insight and scientific fact.) Our personal fears are there to alert us that something needs to change, and by looking at what we actually have with gratitude, we can connect to our power to change. I know the gratitude idea sounds almost too simple to be true, but if you just take a moment right now and think of two or three things you're grateful for, I promise you your mood will improve and your day will get better.

Change starts in the now, so our perspective must see exactly what's true now. And if you want to change your unhappy emotional state, you can't stay stuck about the past and what you don't have, because—it's logical—you can't start building anything on top of what you don't have; that would be starting with nothing.

Perspective—seeing the relationship of things near and far—is a choice we can learn how to make. It means giving up childish self-importance and seeing a grown-up potential in the future. It doesn't come naturally; we have to practice and learn to make it a habit in our lives. If you have the childish habit of complaining, that's a signal that you've either given up your power to choose—too many bad breaks have broken you—or you're afraid that if you choose poorly, things will get worse. I know that what I'm prescribing with this gratitude prescription can sound way too simple. And at some level, of course it's way too simple! Yet . . .

at another level, IT IS that simple. It's one of those weird oxymoronic mysteries that just is. You really have nothing to lose, so why not begin a practice of sincere gratitude every day, and with it an empowering perspective. We always have the *choice* between an intensely personal nearsightedness which sees only me and my emotions or a wider, deeper vision of the world—a realistic perspective that takes into account not just my wants, but everyone who might cooperate with me in getting what I want.

Perspective: use it or lose it.

Sweat This Out

Get out your notebook, jot down numbers one through five, and notice five times in the last week that you lost perspective. Maybe you got impatient or anxious, or the voice in your head started saying "you should"; notice when your thoughts were worries about disasters or obsessing on your inadequacies.

Write down the triggers: You were running late, you couldn't find your keys, something was broken, somebody said something mean to you.

Stop. At the moment you felt the discomforting emotion, what could you control and what did you want that made you crazy?

How could you have redirected your emotional energy into a more realistic perspective—perspective that includes all of your brothers and sisters and not just you and your tribe?

12. HOW MUCH OF YOUR LIFE DO YOU HIDE?

We all have secrets; some secrets are in the past, some in the present. Which of your secrets affects you every day?

If or when or how much you masturbate is probably one of your secrets. But it may not affect much of the rest of your life (assuming you didn't spend your entire morning glued to the porn).

Maybe you shoplifted a bong when you were in middle school. Unless you're still using that bong, chances are it's not having much effect on your life today.

On the other hand, if your coach in middle school track got you high and sexually assaulted you, it may affect you every time you get high with someone you don't know well or even just when you're alone with a powerful person you know is attracted to you.

Or what if, when you were twelve, you stole $150 from your mom's stash. On the one hand, maybe you've fessed up and told her that you were the culprit. In that case, it's likely you and she no longer think much about it. On the other hand, maybe that first bit of thievery has turned into a lifetime habit of skimming. You got away with it then, and you continue to steal packs of paper from work, tips off tabletops, you wear a new pair of shoes out of the store, small items at the grocery store wind up in your pockets . . .

27 QUESTIONS TO MAKE YOU SWEAT

Often our secrets are keys to understanding ourselves. Secrets typically remain secrets because we repress them from ourselves, refusing to even think about them—which is a way we defend ourselves from their emotional unease. By refusing to look at events when we were shamed or embarrassed or we did something we knew was wrong, we think we've put those emotional zombies in a footlocker with padlocks and chains on it. But the zombies are still kicking and screaming inside the footlocker and want to get out. We drag that footlocker full of secrets around and pretend that we can't hear the zombies screaming.

It's time to unpack the zombies and put them out of their misery!

> My sister was home from college for a few days. She and I were in the kitchen making breakfast.
>
> "I can't believe it—as I was coming home, I saw Dad driving a cab in New Rochelle."
>
> "Come on, Lizzy, there's no way that's possible."
>
> "Gregg, I saw him; I know it was him."
>
> "You were probably high and just thought you saw him."
>
> "I was not high. I know what I saw, Gregg. He even looked at me for a second. But then he turned away, like he was ashamed."
>
> "He's busy seeing patients. Why would he be driving a cab?"
>
> "You can't laugh this off. Your father's driving a cab."
>
> "I'm going to ask him."
>
> "Oh right, you think he's going to tell you the truth? We don't have a phone because he hasn't paid the bill. There's no food in the house. Your father is not seeing patients anymore. Your father is driving a cab."
>
> "How can he be driving a cab? He goes to his office every day."
>
> "He pretends to go to the office because he's a failure and

12. How Much of Your Life Do You Hide?

can't admit it. He can't ask for help. Your father just wants to bully you with his pretend psychoanalyst bullshit."
"Why do you keep saying 'your father'? He's your father, too."
"No, I disown him! You think he's acting like a father? I don't. He's hiding the truth from you, from Mom, from himself. I can't live with that. You need to wake up to reality."
"Yeah, well, I still live here. What am I supposed to do?"

After my dad sabotaged his career as a therapist with unethical and illegal acts—a web of secrets—he began driving a cab. But it was a secret he kept from his family. He didn't say a thing until Lizzie hipped me to his charade; he finally came clean and stopped pretending to "go to the office."

But he still hid his Big Secret: his drinking.

After Lizzie left for college, we started finding empty vodka bottles scattered around the house—in closets, under beds, and behind the pillows in the couch. There was no denying the amount of vodka bottles; somebody was obviously drinking a lot of vodka, and only my dad was slurring his words. So we all knew Dad's secret, but the weird thing was, he couldn't admit he was an alcoholic. And we couldn't admit it either. Dad's secret was a huge part of our lives, yet because he had to pretend, we pretended too. But all the pretending and repressed emotion gave all of us a kind of permission. We weren't responsible. The zombies were screaming, but we were turning a deaf ear. It got worse and worse, until one night he smacked my mom and went to jail.

Pretending had become too dangerous; we saw my father's zombies and couldn't repress our emotions any longer. We all began to adjust our lives with a new understanding that, as Lizzie said, he wasn't really a father any longer. Three days after he went to jail (the local police jail), he was out of the house, and for the most part, he was out of our lives from then on. I'd see him occasionally after that, but my trust in him was gone. I could no longer pretend he wasn't an alcoholic and that was the role he'd chosen to live by.

Yet he kept up the act for years, refusing to admit he was an alcoholic. From time to time he'd claim he'd found God and acknowledged his weakness and addiction, and he'd get sober . . . for a while. But it never lasted. After rehab, after riding the wagon for a few months, he'd start with wine, claiming he was a "social drinker," but it wouldn't be long before his life path was littered with more empty vodka bottles.

I could see that my dad's secret was his greatest fear—that he needed the booze to replace his sense of responsibility. If he had been able to admit he was an alcoholic and truly stay sober, he might have built himself back up. He might have regained our trust and redeveloped trust in himself. He might have discovered what he was truly capable of—he really was a brilliant man when he was sober. Instead, his footlocker of repressed zombies kept him a mystery from himself.

We might have been able to help him if he'd trusted himself and us enough to honestly say what was really happening. Yes, he would've had to feel the shame of his unethical behaviors, his inability to support his family, but OK, that's the truth, and you can improve on truth. You can't improve on anything if you're building on secrets and lies—all those screaming zombies, all that repressed emotion.

Decades after that afternoon when Lizzie had seen him driving the cab in New Rochelle, Dad took off for a "new life" in the Philippines. My uncle dropped him off at the airport, and he told me on that very day my dad was slurring his words, almost certainly sloshed. A seventy-nine-year-old man so terrified by the

12. How Much of Your Life Do You Hide?

secrets everyone else knew that he had to fly halfway around the world to escape the evidence.

My dad is an extreme example, but hiding the truth about yourself will always create mistrust and poison relationships. Yet because you're ashamed, you'll tell yourself it's "natural" to push down those memories and emotions until it's a habit. But if you feel insecure and dissatisfied, if you can't succeed to your own satisfaction, if you feel you're always having to prove yourself, it's because you've hidden some key piece of you—not just from others, but from yourself as well.

Not every secret is shamefully toxic, yet if you know there's a part of your life that you have to expend energy and effort to conceal—abuse in the past, war crimes, violence, addictions, felonies, a lie you must maintain—you are undermining your ability to be present and happy with yourself.

This is not to say you should share your secrets with the person sitting next to you on the flight to Denver. Instead you might find an appropriate person, someone who won't judge you, who will listen to you with open and compassionate ears so you can re-experience those feelings in a safe environment. If that seems like too much, you can also write about them in a notebook no one will ever find or simply say them out loud in private. If you're feeling a little braver, you can use the voice memo on your phone just to have the experience of talking out loud about something you've kept hidden.

Here's the kicker: the more you know yourself—the more you can tell the truth about your secrets—the less power shame will have over you. You recover your self-esteem when you admit that you're hiding—and as you come out from hiding, you're able to know, trust, and love . . . first yourself, then other people.

Sweat This Out

Get out your notebook and draw two lines down the page so you have three columns. Leave some room for brainstorming or free association.

In the first column list three big secrets that you've never told anyone. In the second column write down goals that you've wanted but have never reached: weight loss, a sales quota, writing a book, starting a business, committing to a relationship. In the third column write down three distractions; porn, Facebook, Instagram, YouTube, online shopping, gambling, video games, even television if it's always the same story.

Draw lines between secrets, goals, and distractions. Lines might make multiple connections. Use the empty space on the page to make brief notes about a story that could explain why your lines connect. Don't worry if you feel like you're making things up—tell a good story.

13. DO YOU EVER TALK ABOUT DEATH?

If you want to develop a deeper connection with someone—a lover, a friend, a family member, or even someone you find interesting but haven't yet spent time with—consider a conversation about death. It's not a first-date conversation, maybe not even a fourth-date conversation, but pick a serious moment and ask a question. People love questions. Even about death.

In the Sphere of Fear, death—and the many questions you might have about what death might mean—is an impolite topic. It's just not talked about. Or if it is, it's often part of a religious system. But religious answers to any question about death are predetermined, and predetermined answers prevent conversation. You may have feelings or thoughts about death that a predetermined answer doesn't quite get to. It's not a break with your faith to be curious.

Because we know that eventually all of us will have to die—at least in this body—that's one point everyone can agree on. Death will be a reality for all of us, and it requires us to be realistic, not idealistic. We're not talking about *after* death, but the death of this life. That death has many guises and processes; it comes fast or slow, it can happen suddenly, in the prime of life, or through long sickness and old age. The end of one's living, breathing existence affects not just the deceased, but everyone around them. However, in the Circle of Love—unlike the Sphere of Fear—this universal truth is given attention and conversation, maybe even preparation.

> I was at Starbucks when I noticed the guy next to me reaching for the little packets of golden goo. It made me curious: "Honey in your coffee? That's a new one."
> "Trying to get off the sugar." He stirred in two packets.
> "I hear you," I said. "I don't put any sweetener in my coffee at all."
> "That's what I'm trying to get to," he said with a smile.
> "I'm trying to live to 120, so I gotta be cool with the sugar."
> "Wow, I'd be happy with seventy-five at this point." He didn't look more than fifty to me.
> "Seventy-five is hardly old at all!"
> "My good friend just died at sixty," he replied.
> "He was almost a teenager!"
> "Yeah... at the end he wasn't feeling that young, but..."
> "We're all going at some point, so you might as well enjoy honey in your coffee because who really knows when it's our time?"
> "I was there in the hospital when he died, and after all he'd been through—and believe me, he'd been hurtin'—there at the end, he had this huge peaceful smile like, 'It's all OK.'"
> "That's about as good as it gets, leaving with peace and happiness."

This conversation presents two useful life-lessons we can learn by talking about death; one is practical, while the other is more abstract. The first point is simple, and maybe it seems obvious; a long life is valuable, and we should live our lives to protect and extend our life force. All we ever really have is time, and we

13. Do You Ever Talk About Death?

should use our time to buy more time. My coffee buddy and I agreed about cleaning up the sugar nastiness; it tastes good, but it's hell on your endocrine system. By using time to think, to support each other, we may buy ourselves a little more time.

The second lesson is about accepting death. Most of us live as if we're never going to die. But if you accept the absolute certainty that you will die—as we both were able to do in the space of our conversation—then you may grasp the importance of happiness in this moment. Now is the only moment you will ever have, whether you die in five minutes or in ninety years. Now is it . . . FOREVER.

My coffee buddy's friend passed peacefully, happy and accepting. My new acquaintance and I could share a sense of the importance of that feeling and making it a life goal.

A key part of what we ignore when we *don't* talk about death is that each of us dies alone. The journey of death, whatever it turns out to be, is a solo journey. People can be with us at death's door, like my coffee buddy was with his friend, but we have to walk through it alone. We die as individuals, and recognizing that I will die alone tells me that my life has been about my individual purpose, which my death will end, and it was different from anyone else's purpose. So a valuable question to ask, as an individual, is: What is my purpose in life?

You'll notice that usually this question gets asked in philosophical or religious contexts, and another question is: "What is the meaning of life?" But typically the answers are generalizations that apply to everyone. Possible generalizations include: To enjoy myself (aka, to live "the good life"). To raise a family. To contribute to society. To love and serve God.

But generalizations aren't always useful. From the point of view of *your death*: What will stop when you die? What projects or relationships have you been working on that will end with your death? Now you can look back and see your purpose in life. If you die tomorrow, what were you doing you today? You'll notice that your life is full of purpose (or purposes) that your death will put in perspective.

Yes, making healthy eating choices and regular exercise will preserve your life force, and those are reasonable purposes. They are not the full-on reason to be alive, but it helps to see your life purpose in increments. You can make clearer, more positive choices if you see the whole chessboard. Pawns are important—diet, exercise—but what else is going on in the game? Family. Career. Relationships. Those are your king and queen.

Each of us is purposed around those categories—they're the Big Three—yet we often take more time and attention to planning our workouts or meals than we do to carefully considering the details of those more important purposes. *If you knew for sure you were going to die tomorrow, what things would you be doing differently today?* That's a question you might discuss with someone in your family or someone with whom you have a relationship or with someone with whom you have a business.

The point of any discussion is to allow feelings and ideas that are normally stuck in our heads to get loose in the world. This discussion—unlike most conversations in life which just create agreements—is to think out loud without knowing answers and compare beliefs and experiences. Talking about death in this way gives us a chance to notice where we might be stuck in certain religious or cultural dogma we've been raised with. It gives us a chance to see beyond the dogmatic habits we have, and to notice that habits don't change themselves. Like an addiction to sugar, for instance.

The problem with death is that our habits of conversation prevent us from talking about it until someone has actually died.

13. Do You Ever Talk About Death?

And then when we do talk about death, we focus on the person who has died and don't talk about our own relationship to death. When we talk about someone else's death, it's often congested with sentiment and fear. By having a free and open discussion, a lot can be gained, because it can help us to get in front of our sentiments and fears.

Another conversation to have about death is how you want to approach it. It's a'comin'; you need to prepare. If you don't have a will, no matter how young you are or how immortal you think you are, your death will leave problems for people you care about. Have you written your will? A will is fairly simple to make, and it also wouldn't hurt to have a conversation with your heirs about it. If you're young, do you want your parents to be your sole heirs? Do you know what happens if you don't have a will?

The point is simple: talk to the people you care about, and together figure out not only where your stuff will go, but also what kind of send-off you want. What do these people think would help them celebrate your life as they say good-bye? How do you imagine the party or funeral or memorial that would be perfect for you? Yes, it's up to you, but you can create a loving sense of intimacy while you're alive by inviting your friends and loved ones to help.

Possibly a different conversation to have is to ask your intimates about the door of death. What do they imagine happens when we go through the door? We're going to leave this world, and no one knows for certain what's beyond. Even the most devout atheist has to acknowledge that nature is conservative: energy or matter never just vanish—they transform. Our life force is an energy; where does it go?

Essentially death is one of three "logical" doors. One door opens on nothing. One door opens into an infinite "life in the afterlife," and the third opens into a new cycle in which the energy of the departed spirit returns to the material world.

So, for those lucky contestants who chose Door Number One, this life is it. The usefulness of life is exactly what we do in *this life*, and there's no other meaning: done deal. Death is the end.

If that's your belief, then there's no need to waste time debating the possibility or meaning of an afterlife. Some of these people call themselves "atheists," and certain religious practices, such as Zen Buddhism and some Jewish traditions, see the wisdom of focusing on the here and now of this material existence and not confusing things with what might be over the rainbow. It's worth mentioning that the Door Number One group, when compared to those who select the other two doors, live more consistently moral lives. For them, there is no one else to answer to; responsibility begins and ends with an individual sense of right and wrong, not in potential relationships with unseen forces or capricious deities.

Door Number Two usually exists in the monotheistic religious traditions. These folks believe as part of their fundamental dogma that death is a doorway to a new spiritual dimension, and the departed spirit goes on to "a life in the afterlife." The picture of what this "afterlife" is like is usually specific to each religion. Some religions regard this life in the material world like an SAT test: the moral quality of the choices we make in this life will determine where we're qualified to spend our afterlife—heaven, hell, purgatory, and variations on those ideas. As we go through the door of death, our life test is instantly scored, and we will be sent to the campus that best fits our life's choices.

Religions often advise that certain behaviors open the doors to heaven or hell and these behaviors apply to everyone equally.

13. Do You Ever Talk About Death?

But not everyone has the same fundamental problem set in going from cradle to grave. It's all golf, but not everyone gets the same set of golf clubs—in fact, we don't even play on the same course. Some people get caddies and wonderful green courses to hit on; others are stuck alone in the Gobi Desert wondering where the hole is. Life, and all its problems—where you're born, what kind of opportunities you have, what part luck or fate has in determining your pain or pleasure—is all part of "the plan." Which is still the test by which everyone—every different soul—gets one chance at "salvation" or "damnation." One life, one death, and then . . . the door opens and. . . . Did you get into Princeton or are you going to online classes in Attica? FOR ALL ETERNITY! Or did you get to be king or queen of your own special planet with a slave army to serve you?

Door Number Three opens onto the possibility that the spirit and the physical body are in a constant cycle of re-creation, death, and rebirth. An *incarnation* means "put into flesh"—after a spirit-incarnated being dies, the spiritual essence, the soul, goes to another material incarnation. As is true with other belief systems, this soul yearns for a certain perfection, but unlike the heaven or hell traditions above, the soul evolves by a series of incarnations, moving from one level of consciousness to another depending on the choices and the degrees of difficulty in the course of each particular incarnation. Doors Number One and Two open only one way, and they lock behind you. The door of reincarnation is a revolving door. To go back to the golf metaphor: in this model, each soul gets to take many different bags of clubs on many different kinds of courses. The different bags of clubs and the different courses over many rounds (lifetimes) teach the same soul different lessons. The goal is to become an increasingly better player until every shot on every course is a hole-in-one and your spirit has learned all the lessons that materiality can teach. At that point there's no more need to be incarnated in the material world, and your soul (consciousness) has mastered the final lesson: the material world itself is an illusion.

Being able to envision our eventual death is a gift. It's a first step in wondering about where meaning comes from. How you choose to think about what's behind death's door is a choice. And it's a pivotal choice. Coming to grips with the certainty of death and making it part of your consciousness, conversation, and preparations can improve your peace and stability while living inside this physical body. There is no religious or spiritual matrix that can, with 100 percent certainty and evidence, reveal what or if anything happens when we die. The only fact we know for certain is that we are alive now and sometime in the future we will die. The more we can accept the physical death part and rid our self of fear around this issue, the more we can envision our death as a culmination of our life purpose—and the more we can focus on and enjoy the alive-now part!

13. Do You Ever Talk About Death?

Sweat This Out

Write your will—even if you're young. There are will forms on the internet; download one. Prepare for your death by helping those who might survive you. A will isn't only about who gets your stuff; it's about what happens to your body. Your will also can include a statement, a last chance to tell those you love how much you are grateful for their contributions to your life.

Also, and very important: your will should include a "living will" page with your directives about what sorts of measures you want taken if you need to be kept alive on life support.

This is your time in the here and now to stand at an imaginary death's door and turn the knob, and before you step through the doorway, to imagine looking back and saying good-bye.

14. HOW DO YOU RESPOND WHEN SOMEONE ARGUES WITH YOU?

Do you have to "win" every argument? Or do you run and hide out, avoiding arguments and confrontations, even though you know you're right? Or does it depend on the argument and who you're arguing with?

In the Sphere of Fear, you will feel one of two reactions: fight for your side of the argument no matter what or run and hide to avoid all confrontation. In the Circle of Love, we see the problem, not the person; even if our emotions are aroused, we try to solve the problem without attacking the person we're arguing with.

> *"I don't know what I want to do!"* Jessica's voice burst out in frustration. She and I had been talking about living together and writing a performance piece together.
>
> I thought I was being reasonable. *"I'm just saying if we want to try it, we'll need to put some energy into it."*
>
> *"I can't handle this right now! It's too much. I can't take it! Please stop talking to me. I already have too much on my mind!"* she said, as she stormed out of the room and slammed the door.
>
> Ouch. She didn't talk to me for the rest of the night.
>
> The next morning, while she was making coffee, I asked if she was still feeling the pressure.
>
> *"What pressure?"* she said with a smile.

27 QUESTIONS TO MAKE YOU SWEAT

My brother had a different strategy:

Scott and I were on the phone. I was struggling to understand his logic: "So you're claiming the only reason people get God in their life is because they're not happy?"

"Yeah, it's one of the main reasons."

"OK, so what about other reasons? What other reason might turn a person to spiritual practice?"

Scott exploded. "Who needs some fucking spirit thing? I don't need to be saved by a two-thousand-year-old man who never existed. I don't need that fantasy. God is for weaklings and idiots."

"I'll try not to get too offended by that, since after all you're the one who talks about suicide."

"So you think God will save me from suicide? A world full of whiny weaklings clinging to the idea of their God is just another good reason for it."

"My bad. I just don't understand why you're so angry with me if I care enough about you to share a part of my life that makes me happy."

"Who's fucking angry? Are you accusing me of being angry when you treat me like I'm an idiot?"

"OK, I'm not saying anyone's an idiot here, I was just . . . if there's something missing inside of you, that life isn't giving you . . . I was just reaching out from my experience . . ."

"Gregg, I'm not gonna get into this fucking bullshit with you. You're a broken record, and I'm gonna get off because you are fucking BORing. We don't see things the same way; we never will. I accept that; you don't. I will never see the "beautiful light shining through life" the way you want me to see it. EVER! I will DIE before that happens."

He didn't bother saying good-bye.

14. How Do You Respond When Someone Argues with You?

Both situations were similar: I brought something up that pushed emotional buttons and arguments ensued. When Jessica's emotions were triggered, she flared up, but then, rather than try to solve the problem, she simply shut down and checked out. On the other hand, when my brother felt his emotions come into play, he became confrontational and belligerent. Again, he only saw his "unsolvable" problems and my ideas as "fucking bullshit." He tried to make me angry, and failing that, he declared victory and hung up.

Jessica, Scott, and I hit flashpoints of disagreement that caused emotional escalation, which we might call an "argument"—an emotional disagreement. But each of them had strategies for covering up their fears and preventing an emotional de-escalation from turning into a discussion. In both cases, I had something I wanted, and I thought I was being reasonable, trying to turn toward de-escalation and discussion.

But was I really being reasonable?

Yes, Jessica did habitually just shut out any unwanted pressure or emotion—it didn't matter if it was me or some other life situation; she was a runner. By the same token, Scott always finds a reason to be angry. He doesn't need me for him to get pissed off; he has the plumber, the car wash guy, his accountant, our parents, the government—it doesn't matter if it's Republican or Democrat, Scott's an equal opportunity bitchass. But he never wants to go from the problem to facts or ideas; he's all about how inconvenienced or fucked-over Scott is. So yeah, in my life, I'm not entirely reconciled to either Jessica or Scott, and I recognize them as being examples of people who have very powerful habits when arguing, and I notice that they are at the extreme ends of the argument spectrum. Let's keep that in mind.

But if I believe that love is powerful enough to find a way to meet just about anyone halfway, I have to look at my own part in this; was I really separating my feelings from my ideas? Was I really trying to discuss the problem and not—in some way—aggressively confront the person?

That's harder.

I have to admit that I wanted Jessica to agree with me and work with me. I'm not sure I really took the time to acknowledge that she was feeling hassled and overwhelmed. I didn't take that time because I had very definite ideas about what I wanted, and if she would just agree with me, then both our lives would both be better. That seemed so reasonable to me. But I skipped that moment of recognizing how hassled she felt, and then, I didn't really acknowledge that *maybe* what I wanted wasn't "reasonable." I never made the space for all of her feelings, nor did I fully consider what she was saying *she* wanted.

I'm looking back on it now, not to beat myself up, but to learn for the future. If I really want something, I need to tune in to another person's emotional state and let them know that I can see how they're feeling before I put out my wants and needs—which, duh, might be problematic. Also, can I *discuss* in words, exactly what they're telling me that they want? Discussions come from a desire for clarity. Arguments come from venting emotions. It's a difficult lesson, learning to calm down my own emotional reactions and observe someone else's emotional state, taking the time to see what they want—especially when their emotion is hiding an aspect of what they really want.

The key part of this is not letting emotions take us out of ourselves into argument, but recognizing that the surge of emotions are fight-or-flight propositions: once they engage for both people, no one will "win."

The truth is that while emotions are connected to our ideas

14. How Do You Respond When Someone Argues with You?

and beliefs, they can ignite our more immature selves. We have to step back from the emotional fire and let the light of our energy shine on our ideas.

If you're going to get what you want (the reason you're having the argument), that means change; for anything to change, most of the time an argument must turn into a discussion. A discussion is a zone where neither person is taking things too personally. Instead of winning the argument, the intention is to ask how you are feeling, why you are feeling that way, and what you actually need. The discussion has to be grounds for empathy, not antagonism.

It's possible that Jessica and I were just a bad fit, and nothing would have changed that. We could sincerely try for the emotional common ground, but in the end, I don't think we were ready to agree about both wanting the same thing. It happens.

With Scott, arguing had become a habit: when we talked, he would complain about his life, I'd feel bad that my brother was so unhappy, so I'd share my ideas about what makes me happy—and then he'd resent me for being so happy and condescending . . . Oy.

I was just trying to find a way to "make it better," and what has made me happy is the profound sense that God is with me. My side of the conversation was the truth of my ideas—without connecting with the truth of his emotions.

And when his truth got ignored, he'd just get angrier and more unhappy.

It would take more calm and awareness than I had back then to just let it go and say, "Scott, you tell me you're unhappy, and it makes me sad. Is there anything you need from me? But I will love you even if you're unhappy." And leave it at that.

It's still hard to see the ones you love suffer and not try to help.

But in many cases, if "helping" means insisting that "your insight" is correct, it will only perpetuate the arguing. Scott felt so pushed away by my "insight" about spiritual joy that now he barely speaks to me. When we do speak again, I'll have to calm my ass down and let him be happy or sad in his own way; I'll have to withhold any "loving wisdom" and listen hard to how he's feeling when he tells me about those customers who irritate him so much.

And if he asks me how I am, can I tell him honestly without trying to recruit him?

Arguments can be an opportunity for intimacy if they can transform into discussions. A key skill for being intimate is to have an effective process for making that transformation. If I'm going to get to a discussion with Scott, I'll need to be calm with his emotions and mindful of my own emotions.

Mindfulness is the ability to be consciously present with my emotions. I mindfully observe that I am not my emotions, but I am my intention. My intention is to create change in this dialogue, and until I feel like I *could* change, like I understand the other person's internal logic, our emotions will still be exploding all over the discussion.

When I don't have to "win" or "be right," if I can open up so I understand the other person's feelings and fears, and possibly even express my own fears, then we can come to an understanding. Most likely neither of us is totally correct, but we can connect with each other. Instead of having upsetting emotions, we can feel love and respect for each other. This kind of mindful attention isn't "natural"—we are born into and live in a culture that says we must protect our precious ego-identities—yet mindfulness is a skill set that can be learned through practice. We can develop an awareness that emotional fighting isn't going to change anything. No one grows in love or intimacy from an angry argument.

14. How Do You Respond When Someone Argues with You?

Some of us, including me at times, mistake passionate arguing for intimacy. (For example, I think that's what was going on with Scott and me.) Arguing passionately can be a way of playful wrestling: an engagement when we mindfully trace our passions to their sources and expose who we really are in what we believe. Then we can agree to disagree, embrace, and have another drink.

Politics, some points of law, government, art, literature, and philosophy—these are all areas that can invite emotional arguments, and that could prove to be productive discussions if we can keep a focus on the ideas and not on the other person. Empathy, not emotion.

In any relationship that involves personal communication, conflict will inevitably arise. Conflict is one of the most natural aspects of human interaction. And as the tender beings that we are, we need to have skills to protect ourselves—and our *selves* extend into our ideas, our goals, and our beliefs. Figuring out how to handle disagreements gracefully, without launching into an argument or running away from them, is one of the most important skills we can learn.

Sweat This Out

As you get ready to transform arguments into discussions, you'll need to sharpen your awareness of emotional triggers. Get out the notebook, number from one to three, and try to recall three events that created uncomfortable emotions in you. Write down how you felt at that time. We all experience a spectrum of emotions every day. We might feel pleasure from the flavors of breakfast or irritation over having forgotten to buy eggs and bread. Your mission is to notice. Keep in mind that you probably move from pleasure to pain, or from interest to irritation. Emotions have a swing to them.

So pay attention.

The point is: *see your emotions*. Notice that they have triggers. Write down what happened that triggered your emotion. You may see that an emotion gets triggered from a chain of events as much as by just one thing. The road rage you feel may seem to be triggered by the idiot going 55 in the fast lane, but you're driving home from work after your boss criticized a project you just spent a week trying to make perfect. Write down any connections between your emotional moment and things that happened before and after. Remember, you're learning to see yourself having emotions as opposed to your emotions having you.

15. WITH YOUR ROMANTIC PARTNER, WHEN DO YOU EXPRESS ATTRACTION? HOW DO YOU EXPRESS AFFECTION?

We were newlyweds, and Lena and I were just waking up. She opened her eyes and looked at me.
"How'd you sleep?" I asked.
She had the trace of a smile. "I had the weirdest dream."
"What happened?"
"I was sitting on this rock in the middle of a classroom and all the other kids were playing with their iPads. The teacher came by and handed everybody a wet washcloth, except she handed me a pass to the nurse's office and said I needed to go immediately. I told her I felt fine, but she insisted. I got up off the rock and fell through what felt like a giant bowl of lentil soup. All of the sudden I was outside our place; it was the middle of the day, and I was sewing our initials, G&L, into the headrest from the car."
"Hmm... the headrest? A nurse?"
"I'm ready, Dr. Freud; what does it all mean?"
"Not sure about the rock. Maybe stability? But falling into the giant bowl of delicious soup is your yearning for more of my cooking, and the sewing of the initials in the thing that protects my neck means you're going to love giving me neck rubs forever."
"Is that so?"
"Yeah, at least that's what your unconscious is trying to tell you!"

27 QUESTIONS TO MAKE YOU SWEAT

I reached over and tickled her stomach. We rolled around on the bed laughing and tickling each other.
"So what did you do that you needed a special note?"

What is romantic love? It's an affectionate bond between two people, based on attraction and usually physical intimacy. Our ideas about romantic love cover a wide spectrum of relationships, ranging from flirtation to dating to marriage to a lifelong bond. A romantic love bond seems like an important part of any good life, and oftentimes we perform our ideas about romantic love without considering how or what we're really feeling. Because we think romantic love is natural, we don't take the time to fully understand why we want it, what we think we want to give to it, or what we want to get from it. Instead we have some generalized concepts about sex, excitement, and security that we've gotten from our family, our culture, and the media, but these may not really work. With Lena, for instance, I believed that I really wanted this marriage, and I thought I knew how to express my affection.

In this example both of us were expressing love from our hearts. Neither of us were simply performing the role of the lover because we wanted something. Both of us were daring to do something silly, possibly ridiculous. Lena told me her dream—she trusted me with it—and I wanted to be part of her dream, so I expressed my feelings for her in my "interpretation." We took the opportunity to play together. Play requires both trust and improvisation. It's jazz. Not many people know this, but the word jazz used to be a slang for: "playful sex"—and for some of us it still is.

If you feel you love someone and you perform only formulas of appreciation, that's not really loving. You're wearing the mask of the lover, but you're just playing the part, instead of playing

15. With Your Romantic Partner, When Do You Express Attraction?

with who your beloved really is. Who we really are shows up in dreams—those things that make us a little weird and aren't conventionally attractive.

That was a special morning, but other times, I woke up and wanted sex, so I would start working on Lena to have sex. We had a ritual that usually would end up with sex, but in fact it wasn't always what was she wanted—she was doing it for me because she knew that I felt by having sex with me she would be expressing her love. But I wasn't really being with her in the moment and playing with exactly who she was; I wasn't really expressing my love, but instead my needs, and she wasn't able to express her love, but was doing what she felt she had to do.

Both scenarios had identical outcomes, but one was the expression of love, while the other came from subtle fears. My fear was that if I took the time to really be with her, she might not want to have sex; her fear was that if she didn't give in to my morning erection, I might become moody or angry.

It's often the case that play comes easier early in a loving sexual relationship. Just the fact that we're in bed with a new person, maybe in a new house, makes us feel playful, like we're discovering an uninhabited tropical island; everything is brand-new. The more we wake up together, the more we get set in our ways. We don't see and feel the way we used to. Often our lives become complicated by unresolved emotions—anger, resentment, frustration—and we don't feel the baseline of trust, nor do we feel playful anymore. In any relationship, the recent past is going to color our feelings, possibly blocking potential love with fear: fear that we could be rejected, fear that we aren't appreciated, fear that if we tell the truth or act honestly, it will alienate our partner. And these dynamics apply to all relationships: business partnerships, teams, siblings, parents, friends. Fear compels a certain denial of our own truth in the belief that we're preserving the relationship. But we sacrifice play and ultimately, we may sacrifice the relationship, due to all the unexpressed feelings that have accumulated.

Actress Julianne Moore said, "Love is giving someone the power to break your heart, but trusting them not to." Early in relationships, we happily share power, giving up some but feeling that we get in return; over time, however, there are power shifts as we see each other more, as we make more small adjustments. At various points, we may lose the fun of sharing and discovery and begin to resent each other. Part of a successful relationship is being able to express fears and resentments—an expression of love—and trust that the other person will understand.

The trick, of course, is to express only your feelings without blaming the other person. It's being able to express how you feel without making an accusation. That's hard. I know it's been hard for me. When I've been hurt or felt insecure, I've wanted to blame the other person. But blame made the person defensive. That gets nowhere. If I can stay with my own feelings, if I can own exactly how I feel without accusing, my partner has the freedom to tell me her feelings, and we can get back to mutual sharing. When we don't show what's really in our hearts, but instead insist on blaming someone else, it's not because we don't trust our partners—it's because we don't trust ourselves. We don't trust that we'd still be lovable if we're honest about our real feelings; we don't trust that our naked emotions will be understood; we're afraid we'll be judged and found wanting. So we start to block our expressions and instead play out the role that we think will make everyone feel safe. It's like wearing a costume that doesn't fit; we look like what we think we need to be in order to be lovable. Lena was doing what she didn't always

15. With Your Romantic Partner, When Do You Express Attraction?

feel like doing, but she felt obliged to keep wearing the costume of the affectionate wife.

It's worth pausing to say that we've learned this fear. There are many "teachers" we're not even conscious of: movies and television, Instagram and Facebook, our parents and our religious instruction.

When I began dating, there was the great initial, spontaneous, "This is amazing; oh my God, I've never felt this before. I've never experienced another person this intimately with this sense of discovery." And my partner felt the same way. But eventually there was another side to it that would come along. When we started to say the "L" word, we had to start acting the roles of a committed relationship, exclusivity, and so on. And then this role-playing would start to squeeze out the spontaneity.

Why do we replace playfulness with rules and roles? Fear. Fear that we're not good enough, fear that we're going lose the relationship, fear that our partner isn't good enough for us, fear of family criticism, fear of peer group criticism. These fears will crush the playfulness and curiosity. And these fears are learned.

The roots of how we understand giving and receiving love are entangled in our relationships with our primary caretakers. As children, attempting to get our parents' approval and love, we can easily learn that we should hide our troublesome emotions and pretend to be strong, confident, and agreeable. But the problem is that it's dishonest, and we're not learning real intimacy. You can't blame any parent for wanting an agreeable child. On the other hand, maybe without intending to—or even being aware of it—parents can make us ashamed of our authentic emotions.

This is also true of teachers who want agreeable students. Look at the "good" children depicted on television. There's a message about repressing their confusion, inappropriate curiosity, and naughty impulses. But possibly the most repressive social construct today is the peer group. The pressure to fit in to a constantly connected network of values via Facebook, Snapchat, or Instagram creates an unnatural pressure to conform to the group dynamic. It's difficult for any real emotion to emerge and then be privately held, experienced, and cherished if you're snapchatting everything you eat, every place you go.

Because these are early experiences, as we grow into adult relationships, we can think that it's "natural" to suppress our real feelings and present "acceptable" role-playing to any authority, or anyone with whom we have a love attachment. Untangling these very deep and unconscious reflexes of misguided love that we learned as children and moving toward our more authentic expression can be a lifelong process. As I continued meditating, it helped me see more and more clearly that many of the patterns I was experiencing in my romantic relationships were the same patterns I grew up with. Getting Lena's approval about anything and everything felt just like my need for my father's approval.

Once I learned to observe my impulsive need to "be good" and hide my real emotions, I wished I could magically wipe clean a childhood mired in dysfunction, but of course that's not possible. I've discovered that what is possible—right now—is to make a conscious effort to express love even if it feels like I'm at risk.

Here's an easy love to express: appreciation. If I'm fearful or confused, can I look past the fear and confusion and see something I appreciate? I've been able on more than a few occasions to look past the anxious need to feel approval and tune in to what I appreciate about the other person. That's loving behavior. I can do that now even if I'm feeling insecure.

Where are your opportunities to express love? And you have to practice; you have to prepare yourself ahead of time. If, like

15. With Your Romantic Partner, When Do You Express Attraction?

me, you're working against a history of mixed signals, take time in the privacy of your own mind to sort out some appreciations and gratitude to keep handy. There's psychological research on gratitude: people who have a daily habit of listing things and people they're grateful for are happier, live longer, and feel better connections in relationships. Do you have an attitude of gratitude—or just a lot of your own 'tude?

If you're having trouble feeling love from or for the people closest to you, a possible way out of that pattern is to imagine how you like being shown love. What makes you feel cared for? What makes you feel appreciated? What makes you feel beautiful? What makes you feel wanted? Your partner is different from you, but can you figure out what you could say or do to generate those feelings of care, appreciation, and beauty in them? We all want to feel loved and cared for, and any loving action, no matter how simple or small, can have a positive impact.

If you're willing, you can go one step further with finding ways to express your love.

In his great book *Getting the Love You Want*, therapist Harville Hendrix recommends an exercise learned from his own therapist, Richard Stuart. "Caring Days" is an exercise you do with your partner in which you both agree to listen without judgment; you have a conversation—a playful conversation—and tell each other a range of things that you find pleasurable. This will adjust your attention to what your partner really wants and feels is pleasurable, and you can use the exercise to be able to better recognize opportunities to do those things spontaneously. This way, you don't have to always guess about what makes your partner feel good, and it can be magic if, even when you're not feeling good, you choose to make dinner or offer to do the shopping. You may find that by expressing love, you feel love.

27 QUESTIONS TO MAKE YOU SWEAT

We have a cultural belief that after a certain amount of time in a relationship, you know the other person, and the relationship no longer needs work. But just as plants die without proper nurturing, relationships wither and die when participants fail to communicate and make time for each other. The expression of love is the sunlight and water for a relationship. "The love you make is equal to the love you take" is how the Beatles put it, and it's true: if we want to receive more love in our life—and we usually do—we need to *give* more love in our life. It really is that simple. The not-so-simple part is expressing that love when we feel we've been hurt, neglected, or taken advantage of. Those are all feelings of being unloved. You can cure yourself by choosing to love anyway.

Sweat This Out

Get out the notebook. Two things:

1) Make a conscious choice to make eye contact with and smile at everyone you interact with, and later that day make a note of who you smiled at.

2) Pick a friend, parent, lover, or sibling. Tomorrow you're going to surprise the one you've chosen with an unexpected act of love-a present or activity that will make that person feel good. Any loving action will suffice, from buying a plane ticket to cleaning the kitchen. The size of the gesture is not as important as the love that inspired it. Something is always better than nothing when it comes to expressing our love.

16. DO YOU TAKE FULL RESPONSIBILITY FOR ALL YOUR ACTIONS?

How many of your experiences do you feel you create and how many of your experiences do you believe are controlled by outside forces such as luck, family, the weather, genetics?

"I shouldn't have to be working." My mom was tired after a long day at the store.
"Well, Mom, I'm working too." We all had jobs.
"Your father's not telling the truth. He's making money, but he hides it from me. It's not fair. I shouldn't be working this stupid job."
"Mom. I don't understand why you stay married to him."
"Oh, so I should just get a divorce? Then he really won't support us."
"C'mon, Mom. Are you really happier feeling chained to him with his lies and false promises?"
"He's made life horrible for all of us."
"But, Mom, if he's horrible, we don't have to stay with him. Don't you see? We'd all be happier if you divorced him. What are you afraid of?"
"I don't know what to do. We've been married for more than twenty years."

27 QUESTIONS TO MAKE YOU SWEAT

"It doesn't have to be another twenty."
"It's his fault; he got us into this mess. He should get us out."
"Mom, you have to take control of your life. Don't you see that Dad is still controlling you?"

My mom stayed married to my dad long after she knew he was a danger—to himself, to his clients, and to the most vulnerable of all, his family. Yet she clung to him, afraid to be alone, afraid to take responsibility for herself and her children without having him to blame for her lack of money and power.

I remember that conversation vividly. I was so frustrated with her, and she was so frustrated with him. I urged her to divorce him, but she was so addicted to blaming him for everything that she couldn't even imagine living without him. Plus, the very idea of separating was outside of her belief system. But eventually she faced her massive insecurity and fear of being alone and weighed that feeling against what it felt like being with her crazy and dangerous partner. And when she finally did divorce him, we all felt a new and wonderful sense of liberation.

Why did it take so long? It may have to do with how much of our life we are willing to fully own. Blaming others for our problems lets us off the hook for taking responsibility for those parts of our life that are frustrating or disappointing—we choose to remain in these relationships because we can claim to be the victim. And we're not only victimized by bad relationships; we can be victimized by luck or disease or accidents or errors—anything that makes the story we tell ourselves "not our fault."

How can we be in a realistic and healthy relationship with ourselves when we're constantly telling the story of how someone or something else has made us miserable, or cost us money? How can we gain control of our lives if we keep telling ourselves

16. Do You Take Full Responsibility for All Your Actions?

that *bad things happen to us and it's not our fault?* Consider this: control is forward-looking. If I control the car I'm driving, I'm looking ahead. My attention and intention are forward-oriented. Yet many of us live our lives as if we were driving forward but only looking in the rearview mirror. If I blame my bad feelings, my lack of money, or my lack of love on bad luck or bad people, I'm not really going forward; I'm dwelling in the past. Whenever I tell myself, "It's *their fault*," I'm reliving that past event or relationship instead of owning the outcome of the past event and going forward to create a positive outcome. If I'm going forward, I'm fixing what is with what will be, not fixating on what was.

When people continually rehash the past, they often feel as though they experience the same bad things over and over—"I can't seem to find a good partner," or "I keep injuring myself playing football," or "I always get the worst boss," or "The [insert political party here] want to destroy my country." By blaming others, luck, or circumstances, we fixate on the familiar emotions that are associated with the past problem instead of taking the risk of changing our behavior, which could create uncontrolled emotion. My mom wanted to stay in her familiar dance of resentment with my father rather than boogie away from him and dance to her own music. We can only learn from our mistakes when we accept our responsibility for the error and consciously change the behaviors that contributed to it.

There is a profound difference between blame and responsibility. Blame is a habit of irresponsibility. It's a way of not taking responsibility. When we blame others, it's a way to avoid taking full responsibility for our lives. Instead we protect ourselves with the story that "it's someone else's fault." And in some cases, it could be true that someone hurt us, and it was entirely their fault; they were entirely to blame. Often these situations happen when we're children and don't have a developed self or the power to self-determine. But the responsibility for repair is our own. This doesn't mean that if a hurricane flattens your house, you have to single-handedly rebuild the house using only the debris for materials—but you do need to take ownership of the problem and find out what agencies or help you can get to assist you. Ownership and responsibility are not about taking the blame—it's not your fault the hurricane hit—but they are about taking control of consequences.

By the same token, if you were abused as a child, you need to take responsibility for working through the experience. However, what we know about abuse is that the abused often grow up to become abusers—even as they tell others about how awful it was to be abused. Internally, they blame their need to abuse on their victimhood—they can't control themselves because it's what they've learned. It's the previous abuser's fault.

To create our lives with full responsibility, we have to take ownership of old feelings of victimhood, blame, and powerlessness. The first step is having the courage to look at our lives openly and honestly. When were you victimized? If the hurricane flattened your house or the adult abused you, it's not your fault. Everyone at some point has been a victim. You aren't meant to take the blame, but you will have to take full responsibility for repairing the damage. Until we become conscious of the habitual patterns of blaming, victimizing, complaining that may be running our lives, we won't get out of pain, nor will we experience confidence and being in control of our lives. Full responsibility means getting past blame and getting to solutions.

We have a choice: we can see ourselves as sad and sorry victims of unfairness—or we can see ourselves as blessed creators of our own experience. The first path leads to feeling helpless and resentful; the other leads to empowerment and ultimately to joy.

16. Do You Take Full Responsibility for All Your Actions?

Sweat This Out

Make a list: think of events in your life when "things didn't work out well for you."

These things could include accidents, a broken heart, job loss, family feuds, speeding tickets, times when you were *so close* to getting the job or the deal or the gig . . . but damn, it didn't happen. Be sure to recall both the profound and the trivial—the bad grade in chemistry along with the death in the family.

Go for thirty entries. You can include your second-grade teacher, Ms. Meaniepants, or anything else that still bugs you.

How much of what happened was just "bad luck"—you were just in the wrong place at the wrong time?

How much did you—by attitude, behavior, poor planning, or bad relationships—contribute to this downer?

Which of these events are you still holding on to, still thinking about, still feeling emotion when you replay them?

For those things you still feel emotional about, what are they like in your life today? If you're still angry that a teacher treated you unfairly, who in your life today treats you unfairly? Is it possible there's someone *you* treat unfairly?

17. HAVE YOU AND YOUR PARTNER DEFINED WHAT YOU BOTH WANT IN TERMS OF ROMANTIC COMMITMENT?

From flirting to free love to forsaking all others in every way, have you and your significant other defined your expectations? [If you're not currently in partnership, what are your personal expectations?]

> Lena and I were in the undersized bathroom of our beautiful carriage house. I was flossing my teeth as Lena applied moisturizer to her thighs.
> "I don't understand. Why do you have to talk to him so much?"
> "He's my friend, Gregg. Will you stop being so jealous?"
> "I'm not being jealous, Lena. You've been going to yoga class with him for five months,
> and I haven't said a word. I'm not jealous of you having a guy friend, but I have a problem with you texting a guy friend ten times a day."
> "We text about little things like friends. Since we moved out here in the country, I don't have any friends. Why can't you be OK with that?"
> "It doesn't feel good to me that you need another man to talk to. It hurts me that another man is doing something for you I

can't. Especially when I know he has the hots for you."
   "He just broke up with his long-term girlfriend. Dan's not ready for a relationship."
   "Like that ever stopped anyone! Dan confessed to me that he really, really digs you. You're paying too much attention to him. You're my wife, I'm in love with you, and this hurts me."
   "Gregg, you're so wrong about this. He's my friend; there's literally nothing going on between us. You need to breathe and relax. Everything's going to be OK. I love you, not Dan."

I had been married for only a year when my wife started to see a lot of her yoga teacher, Dan. What Lena claimed was just a student-teacher relationship looked to me like an intimate courtship. At first they called each other, though over the course of several months, they began texting ten or twenty times a day. I hate to admit it, but yeah, I counted. After a day of work, I would come home to find out that she'd been on the phone with him all day and had plans to do yoga with him the next night—just the two of them at his studio. She said that he was her friend and she was helping him heal from his recent break-up.

To this day, Lena would say that the two of them were just "really close friends." To this day, even though we're divorced, Lena still claims that they were only friends. It still looks more intimate than "friends" to me.

At some level, Lena and I couldn't communicate our most complete and honest feelings. Instead, we were withholding our truths and our more authentic feelings in order to have what we believed was an "ideal" relationship; we were enacting our ideas about "marriage." We were doing what we *thought* we wanted, what we thought we could get from each other, because it fit the picture in our heads of marriage. If anything happened that

17. Have You and Your Partner Defined What You Both Want?

wasn't in the picture, it wasn't that important. I had a gorgeous wife, and I felt powerful giving her everything she wanted; she had a musician husband, a great house, a great car—and her own personal yoga boy.

What was wrong with this picture?

We both denied our own truths to maintain that relationship for too long.

Eventually, I came to my senses when she admitted to having sex outside the marriage—we'd gotten as far as marriage counselling—and the guy wasn't even Dan. I had thought I had accepted her need for male attention, so in a way, I wasn't that surprised. It was a mess and wound up causing both of us terrible pain.

But before all that, when we were having the conversation about her texting Dan, on the one hand, I was jealous, but I couldn't say out loud that I didn't trust my wife. On the other hand, my wife—no matter what she was actually doing with Dan—was seeing a lot of a man who had told her husband he wished he could have a relationship with her.

Lena and I were both afraid to tell each other the whole truth. We had a belief that simply maintaining the image of a relationship—she was smart and beautiful, and I was a hip musician in a killer band—was more important than our actual behavior in the relationship. Honest in-depth discussions about our actual behavior and our actual feelings were just too dangerous. They might have generated emotions so powerful that they'd shatter the picture of our perfect romantic relationship.

What is committed behavior? There are two radically different ways of thinking about commitment. On the one hand, traditional ideas about marriage are based on a property model. When we marry, we become each other's property, and No Trespassing Allowed. In this regard a "committed relationship" means no sexual behavior with anyone other than your partner. But to imagine your partner as your exclusive property is to imagine slavery. Yes, they may "agree" to exclusivity, but I doubt if anyone lives as another's property without resentment.

So let's redefine "commitment" as different from property. Instead of ownership, think of a contract. A contract is a conscious agreement between two parties who may have different interests. A contract can be cancelled or renewed depending on the desires of the two parties, and both parties are mutually responsible. At the base of any successful contract is honesty. In the commitment contract I'm proposing, I will communicate my desires as honestly as I can, and I want my partner to do the same with me. As partners, we agree to trust one another even while we have lives that engage with other people.

And other people will be interesting—so this is where you and your partner get to negotiate the issues of trust and temptation. How much do you want to flirt? How much do you want to know about your partner? How comfortable are you telling the truth about your attractions? How comfortable are you hearing about your partner's attractions? This must all be negotiated, and it may not be symmetrical. Is there something you would prefer your partner didn't do?

You agree to limit intimate physical behavior unless you both agree not to. And you will define what intimate physical behavior is to each of you. Remember, you and your partner are the only people agreeing to this contract. It's either an expression of love or an expression of fear. Our desires reveal who we truly are: if I feel free to express (not necessarily act on) my desires, I can feel free and loved. And I will love the person who frees and understands me.

Committed behavior may need to be defined differently

17. Have You and Your Partner Defined What You Both Want?

between different couples, but for all couples the key is *agreement*. Consider that being honest about feelings and fantasies, unacted on, might be OK to talk about and worth putting in the agreement. If you can communicate "dangerous" truths about yourself and feel accepted, that's trust. It's a deeper intimacy than pretending that such thoughts don't exist.

If Lena had just admitted that she was attracted to Dan and that she knew he was hot for her, I might have felt, "OK, that's the truth." But ten texts a day after Dan told me how badly he wanted Lena gave me a nagging pain; I always felt that if I couldn't trust her to be honest with either herself or with me about a fairly obvious reality, then how could I trust her at all? Worse, as much as I was so hurt by her behavior, I didn't trust myself to quit what looked like a great relationship, so I couldn't even trust myself. In a way, both Lena and I had become slaves of a pretty picture of a perfect marriage, but both of us were miserable having to lie about our true feelings to be able to stay married.

If your partner is sharing a laugh with someone else and appears to be having a great time, do you interrupt? Do you feel a jolt of jealousy and hold back, observing and stewing? Can you let it go, or do you wait until later, at home, and then begin a cross-examination or throw a temper tantrum?

Or, if you can engage the commitment contract, can you see that your beloved is having a good time and move on to finding your own good time? Just because she's "on a diet" doesn't mean she can't "look at the menu." That's true for you as well. And if you're not there yet, if you do feel that zap of jealousy, can you at least take full responsibility for your feeling? That would mean waiting for an appropriate time—definitely not at the party—to tell your partner how you felt.

27 QUESTIONS TO MAKE YOU SWEAT

If your partner is doing something that makes you feel jealous, it's your duty to express how you feel without blaming or shaming. Feelings of jealousy range from anger to insecurity to abandonment: in all of these you *imagine* a motivation your partner may not even have, so in expressing yourself, you need to cue your partner with *your* feelings—including physical sensations like "sick to my stomach," "sweating my brains out," "immediate migraine"—but only what *you felt and feel*. To get to an understanding, your mission is to only share the truth of your emotions.

If you want to preserve your relationship, the key is avoiding any accusations. Demanding to know "what's really going on" is one of those deadly accusations. Can you just listen to how your partner feels without judgment or blame? Help yourself with some reality testing: remind yourself that your partner did not enter into that conversation or situation in order to hurt you, so don't turn your insecurity into an accusation. Yes, playful behavior could be serious flirting, which could be a preamble to sex; but playful behavior can also be simply friendly playful behavior—"fun," as they used to call it. And sometimes looking at the menu will give you an appetite for the meal that is on your diet. In that case, the playful conversation you observed might make your partner hot for you later! Also, what if there is an attraction, and then in the intimacy of sharing that attraction, you *both* get turned on? Intimacy mixed with risk—and it can feel risky telling a "dangerous" truth—is exciting!

That won't happen if you start making accusations.

But it's a whole lot easier to make accusations than to take responsibility for exposing your weakness, fear, or insecurity. To tell your partner the truth about those feelings—without adding your judgements about what you imagine was happening—is to make yourself vulnerable.

17. Have You and Your Partner Defined What You Both Want?

In time you may see that your jealousy is just your projection, and you can learn to trust your partner because he or she listens to you and tries to understand. Or, if hurtful things happen over and over again, eventually you will see that *your needs* and *your partner's behaviors* don't match. In that case, you aren't making good, honest connections, and you don't belong together.

Honesty is an index of health. Dishonest relationships will eventually be toxic.

Many times in relationships, we will compromise our emotional truth for a picture of what we *think we want* and try to play a role just to keep that picture. We're afraid that telling the truth about ourselves to our partner will destroy the relationship. Built into that behavior is a belief that even a dishonest relationship is better than no relationship; but c'mon, really? The conversation you need to have is to communicate how you truly feel and get an agreement or understanding about what you both want.

Chances are, if you've been dishonest, your partner has tuned in to that, so when you tell the truth, you'll both feel relieved. And you may find that your attraction is renewed. Honesty can be sexy.

So you and your partner need to define how you will be committed to one another. Commitment happens when both partners keep to their agreements—and some partnerships can agree to more personal freedom and experimentation than others. As you grow more in trust, perhaps you can expand the boundaries and expectations. You may learn that what you thought at the start might not be true anymore, and you can adjust the contract as you go. As long as you stay honest.

To speak openly about what's in your heart with no fear of rejection is what many in the spiritual community call heaven, but really it's love. And just by the way, love isn't like a switch—on or off, you either get it or you don't. Love is like a muscle that we all have. The capacity for love can get stronger with exercise, or even with stress. A strong love may be made stronger by difficulty, by learning to trust, and by learning to tell a truth we think we're afraid to speak.

Sweat This Out

If you're involved in a romantic relationship, do this with your partner; if you're single, do this with a friend.

Discuss what behaviors your partner thinks are reasonable. What kinds of behavior are flirtatious? If your partner thinks a movie star is sexy, is that OK to say? Can you be honest about finding another person attractive? If not, what part of the relationship needs to adjust to accept that very natural attraction? Is it a two-way street?

This is practicing honesty. Just asking probing questions and listening.

You probably want to start with low-risk items, checking in with what you think is fun, interesting, or maybe exciting about your partner's thoughts, and then work up to the powder keg of what you'd rather not know.

And remember, you can always renegotiate.

18. WHAT DO YOU KNOW ABOUT THE BUDDHA?

My drum student Henry came from a relatively normal, middle-class American home. After he had finished his paradiddle exercise, he had asked something about one of the Buddha quotes he'd seen on the wall of my music studio.

Buddha walked the path and figured out how to make paradoxes melt away and put his mind at peace. Buddha found out for himself how to attain peace and happiness. Buddha said, "Believe nothing, no matter where you read it, or who said it, no matter if I have said it, unless it agrees with your own reasons and your own common sense."

"So if I want peace and happiness," Henry said as he hit a rim shot, "I have to believe in nothing?"

"Not exactly. If you know a few simple Buddhist ideas, you might see that they're useful for your happiness. But Buddha's point would be to check any 'belief' you have against your deepest feelings."

"What if I think my belief in God is really important, so then this Buddhist idea is bullshit?"

"Recognize that it's the truth. For you. Now. But recognize that your emotion is fear: people don't use the word bullshit *unless*

they're angry and afraid."
"Bullshit."
"That would be my point."
"I don't feel afraid."
"Really? Then why do you need to curse about my Buddha saying? It seems like you're overreacting. If you were fearless and confident, you wouldn't try to insult me. But it's OK with me if you can't hold the idea that your belief in God is important to you, and also that you may not really need it and still be you."
"You're confusing me."
"It's like a paradox. Paradoxes are when two ideas contradict one another, yet both seem to be true. Instead of wanting to reject something you don't know about, try to just hang out with the concept that paradoxes are, in a crazy way, sometimes real."
"So Buddha says it's OK to reject Buddhism, if . . ."
"If you're willing to know what you're rejecting. If you meet the Buddha, kill the Buddha."
"What the—?"
"It's an old Buddhist saying: 'If you meet the Buddha on the road, kill him.'"
"What does that even mean?"
"It means don't get attached to anyone else's ideas about things. Don't get attached to any words, any forms, any rituals, any person, any anything. The essential Buddhist idea is to know yourself before there are words."

When I was sixteen, the guitar player/singer from my first real band gave me a book entitled *The Way of Zen* by Alan Watts. Watts was sixteen himself when he joined a Buddhist Lodge in London and then devoted himself to understanding religion, in particular Zen Buddhism. *The Way of Zen* was his first major

18. What Do You Know About the Buddha?

book, and it introduced me to a spiritual life that didn't need an overseeing God keeping track of who was naughty or nice, deciding who gets the ultimate Christmas present of heaven or the ultimate Christmas stocking full of hell.

Instead, *The Way of Zen* offered the Buddhist prospect that a spiritual life doesn't depend on "God-given rules," but comes from my own truest sense of right and wrong. In Zen, there is no "Divine Judge" watching over everybody, no sinister Santa Claus keeping a list of sins in order to punish us. The Buddha is not some divine being; instead he serves as an image of me, my own imperfect perfection—free to make errors, but then free to see the truth of how my actions affect others. The responsibility for my life is ultimately mine alone—and that sounded like the most exciting, adventurous philosophy on earth. A universe that had my experience at the center and not some bearded voyeur on a cloud.

I wanted to know more about Buddhism, so I continued reading, and that convinced me to start sitting—which means meditating. However, for modern Western people meditation can be a struggle, since we think we should always be doing something. But meditating as the Buddha taught is "not-doing": "to sit with oneself, alone, without thoughts or desires." It's sitting still, turning off the faucet of ever-flowing thoughts, "the monkey-mind" that's constantly telling me who I am and what I want. That was and is a tall order. But I felt that to be my most authentic me, I had to turn off the pesky thoughts and arrive at an inner silence. So I began sitting, allowing the chatter to die down.

Slowly, over time, sitting has changed me. In fact, there's very good Western science on how regular meditation changes the actual structure of our brains. Through meditation we become more self-aware and less reactive. In brief, we stop reacting to other people's judgments and manipulations; we stop needing their approval and instead come to rely on our own truth and authenticity. In a word, we become centered. I grant you that there's a lot of monkey-mind to sit with—it's not as easy as choosing red or blue, Neo—but eventually it will happen. I don't even know why, but with meditation, I've found that I can grow beyond old ideas of "who I am."

The Buddha spoke of the concept of impermanence as one of the pillars of human life. Our self, our desires, and life itself are all impermanent; we are part of a flow that is always changing, and meditation allows us to feel that flow. It's when we resist the flow—grasping and clinging to things or ideas or roles—that is the cause of our suffering.

The Buddha taught that this existence of ours is as transient as autumn clouds. To watch the birth and death of beings is like looking at the movement of a dance. A lifetime is like a flash of lightning in the sky, or perhaps like a torrent rushing down a steep mountain: it's gone as fast as you can you notice it.

The Buddha was clear that he was a man, not a god, and he came by his spiritual insights honestly, by suffering and meditating; he offered his life as an example of how we all can come to know ourselves and our lives more deeply.

The Buddha could have been a spoiled jackass with servants bowing to his every whim for his entire life. He was born in 566 BCE, the prince of the ruling family in a small kingdom called Kapilavastu. Siddhartha Gautama, the man who would become the Buddha ("the awakened one"), was raised with everything he wanted, and at sixteen he was married to a beautiful princess named Yasodhara.

But Siddhartha was no fool. Although he could see that his life of luxury and beauty was the envy of everyone around him, from

18. What Do You Know About the Buddha?

the servants to the nobility, he felt a deep discontent. Nothing touched him deeply. Nothing satisfied him. He felt like he was performing in a play someone else had written for him.

Frustrated with himself for his indolent ways and the palace life that held only insincere conversations, he stole outside the royal compound in disguise and went among ordinary people to see what life might really be like. He saw things he'd never been allowed to see before: squalor and disease, violence and hatred. He saw petty squabbles and clans hating each other for absurd reasons. He thought, "How can I enjoy my royal life of pleasure when there is so much suffering in the world?"

So he joined a group of wandering monks and studied with the great teachers of the day, trying to find a way of life that was honest yet without suffering. He taught himself not to trust in the appearances of things: wealth, beauty, cruelty, and fear; not to trust the king because he had a title, the rich man because he had money, the priest because he offered a connection to God. The more he studied, the more he became convinced that life held illusions to seduce us away from our most essential selves. Worldly goods, fine food, beautiful women, fast horses, and sweet talk: all of these would inevitably lead to suffering.

Surely the path of happiness was simplicity—seeing and loving only what was essential in life. Siddhartha began to deny himself those things of the world he thought were not essential. Those nonessential things must be the cause of suffering. They were distractions on the path to happiness. Yet, although he "knew" this, he had trouble accepting it as truth. Some part of him liked being distracted. He tried severe asceticism, denying himself food, water, light, and sleep, yet these denials were distractions too.

Siddhartha stopped his studies with the masters and vowed to sit with himself and see what happened. He chose a Bodhi tree and sat for seven weeks without moving from that position until his mind stopped its chatter, his desires for any worldly thing or person evaporated, and he eventually came to a oneness with reality. He became the Buddha, "the Awakened One."

For the next forty-five years, he taught people from all walks of life that attaining enlightenment is a process, a discipline, and it's not attained by following a prescribed belief system. Instead of a complicated belief system, he offered observations that could be true for anyone, and he called them the Four Noble Truths:

> Life is suffering.
>
> Suffering is caused by attachment to things or people.
>
> There is a path to stop suffering.
>
> Here's the way to do it.

Still keeping it simple, Buddha offered eight signposts that show the way to walk "The Eightfold Path," which regulates the eight essential aspects of consciousness:

> Right View—See the world as it is, not as it appears.
>
> Right Intention—Peaceful renunciation of worldly pleasures, the intention of good will toward all sentient beings, and the intention of harmlessness. When intentions are right, actions will be right.
>
> Right Speech—Speak in a truthful but non-harmful way, appropriate to another's feelings.
>
> Right Action—Avoid physically harming another being; don't take what does not belong to you; don't impose your desires on an unwilling person.

18. What Do You Know About the Buddha?

Right Livelihood—Earn your living without doing harm to any sentient being or limiting their freedom.

Right Effort—Keep your mind on honesty and decency toward others; avoid unwholesome qualities or imagining evil deeds.

Right Mindfulness—Try to see the world with clarity, without craving things or status; do not avert your gaze: look at everything, even what makes you uncomfortable or ashamed.

Right Concentration—The mental discipline to unify the mind into one-pointedness focus, often referred to as Samadhi.

When you are on the path, the Buddha said, you will see that the universe is all connected: nothing is lost in the universe, yet everything is constantly changing (in flux). As we live in the constantly changing state of the universe, the law of cause and effect applies to all our actions: if we act from right intention, we will cause good effects; acting from wrong intention, we will create wrong circumstances in this lifetime that will inevitably cause unhappiness, affecting ourselves and others. Our actions create our fate; that's cause and effect. The ancient word for this is Karma. Our actions and choices create our Karma. This is exactly what Jesus meant when he said, "As you sow, so shall you reap." When we do good things, good things (good Karma) come into our life; when we do harm, we experience suffering. Here's an illustration:

A poor widow named Krisha whose only baby had died was inconsolable. She wandered from house to house with her dead son in her arms begging for a way to bring her tiny child back to life. She found the Buddha teaching in the countryside and pleaded with him, "Please, Lord, give me the medicine to bring my child back to life."

The Buddha listened to her pleading and said, "I can help. Go down to the city and bring me back a mustard seed from a home where no one has died."

She was filled with hope and set off to find that household. But as she went from home to home and heard the sad tales of death from residents in every home, she realized what the Buddha had sent her to find: not magic to bring her child back to life, but the truth that suffering is part of life, and we all have to die.

When she returned to the Buddha, he asked her, "Did you bring the mustard seed?"

"No," she said. "I am beginning to understand the lesson you are trying to teach me. Grief made me blind, and I thought that only I had suffered at the hands of death."

"Why have you come back?" asked the Buddha.

She replied, "To ask you to teach me the truth of what death is, what might lie behind and beyond death, and what, in me, if anything, will not die."

"There is only one law in the universe that never changes—that all things change; all beings, all things are impermanent. The death of your child has helped you to see now that the realm we are in—samsara, the daily life—is an ocean of darkness, of unbearable suffering. There is one way, and one way only, out of samsara's ceaseless round of birth and death, and that is the path to liberation. Because pain has now made you ready to learn and your heart is opening to the truth, I will show it to you."

The widow Krisha saw the light and followed the Buddha the rest of her life.

18. What Do You Know About the Buddha?

To become peaceful like the Buddha, we need to develop two qualities equally: compassion and wisdom. Compassion is seeing the world with feelings of love, kindness, mercy, tolerance, and charity. Wisdom includes a thoughtful understanding of the Four Noble Truths, the Eightfold Path, and the action of Karma. The Buddha also warned us not to develop our emotional side while neglecting our rational side; we may become kind-hearted fools, easy to manipulate. On the other hand, if we neglect our ability to experience our feelings, we may turn into a coldhearted cynic incapable of heart-to-heart connection.

The Buddha taught silent meditation as the best way for each of us to find and pursue the light. If we learn to gradually silence our mental chatter, we will see the world as it is. We can detach our egos from things and beliefs and feel the peace of living without fear, without desire. We all have the Buddha nature within us: we can, if we calm our desires and fears, see the world in its constantly transforming flow.

Spending some of your precious time in meditation is a way to understand suffering for what it is: a choice, *your* choice, the result of the laws of cause and effect. I know that if you're in pain right now that is the last thing you want to hear. "Wait a damn minute, why would I *choose* to feel this hurt, to be crippled, impoverished, alone in the world?"

Perhaps you didn't see those things coming, but who you are is the net result of choices you've made, the *causes* you have chosen. Meditation is a method to still your mind so that those causes may become clear. Seeing the choices that have caused your suffering is the first step to alleviating suffering. If you can take the first step, you are on the path to happiness.

Many people have the idea that true happiness is for some

future time, but the Buddha taught that happiness is not in the future; it is right now. He said, "Pain is certain; suffering is optional."

Sweat This Out

Sit with nothing going on; this is basic meditation. Set an alarm to a soft tone, and simply sit for five minutes.

You needn't be bolt upright, but a straight spine is what the hardcore Zen-types sit with.

Close your eyes or keep them half-open, fuzzy-focus on a point right in front of you.

Just breathe.

Put your attention on your in-breath, then your out-breath. Let go of thinking. Become your body breathing. It's completely OK to feel as if your head is empty.

If your mind must have something to do, try counting slowly to four on the in-breath, then at the same pace, count to ten on the out-breath.

Try not to move and keep counting until your alarm jingles. Notice how you feel.

One thing is certain, whatever pain is bothering you will show up and monkey with your thoughts. That's OK. Can you calm your thoughts and let it be? Do a four-count inhale followed by a ten-count exhale. There's good research showing that a prolonged exhale—two or more times longer

18. What Do You Know About the Buddha?

than the inhale—shifts body systems into a more relaxed, hormone-healthy state.

Five minutes. Simple.

Sitting gets easier and easier each time you do it. When you can sit without moving, just breathing for five minutes, try ten.

If you can sit for ten minutes a day for thirty days in a row, your blood pressure will drop. You'll sleep at night. And . . . well, see what happens to your pain.

19. WHAT DO YOU KNOW ABOUT JESUS?

You probably have one of two responses to that question: either "Jesus is God made flesh, an example for all mankind" or "I don't deal with that Jesus stuff."

Those responses are your experience up to this moment.

How about if you hang with Jesus without judgments or any religion and approach him with a friendly and philosophical lens. Maybe some history, some psychology, but most definitely not as a test of your personal beliefs.

Which is to say, let's look at the story.

> I was lost in the metaphysical section of Barnes & Noble. I had picked up a book about the "teachings of Jesus" and started leafing through it. A college-aged kid, inches away from me, poking through his own choices in the dizzying array of metaphysical titles, turned to me as I was honing in on one of the passages in the Jesus book and asked me a question.
>
> "Who knows if Jesus even existed?"
>
> "You mean Jesus? The real guy Jesus?"
>
> "Yeah, what if there was no real guy Jesus?"
>
> "OK, let's say he didn't exist, no historical Jesus. But the effects of a character named Jesus in a book called the New Testament do exist. Do you agree that there are real effects of

this character?"

"Yeah, it's kinda hard to deny."

"For me, it doesn't matter if the character Jesus was a real man or not. What matters are the stories and the moral lessons I can get from the stories. The Jesus story teaches us how each one of us can have Christ Consciousness. The Bible stories are there so we have a model, this character named Jesus, as an example of a good man. As I develop my Christ Consciousness, I find that goodness flows more naturally from me. And the good news is that anybody can do it."

"So you're saying it doesn't matter if there was a historical Jesus or not?"

"For me personally, yeah, I think there was a guy named Jesus who walked among us. But I don't think it matters. I'm all about the effects of the teachings."

"So does this Christ Consciousness mean you have to follow all those religious rules?"

"For me anyway, Christ Consciousness is about a philosophical openness to feeling my—or your—connection to the divine. Christ Consciousness isn't about being a good rule follower or having all your friends call you a 'good Christian.' Maybe that's the difference between religion and philosophy. Religion is about the rules. Philosophy is about each person thinking critically about life and learning to make better choices. The story of the Christ is about a dude who woke up to his own connection to the divine and wanted to share it."

"Yeah, but the 'divine' means like God or something, so you're back to religion and believing in God?"

"Not necessarily. The story of Jesus Christ helps us see that the divine is the feeling of connection. Connection is what Christ Consciousness is all about. It's the consciousness of connecting

19. What Do You Know About Jesus?

to other living beings, to the natural world, to our own talents and perceptions, to ideas that demand something of us. Jesus' stories show us ways to activate our connections by loving, seeing beauty, feeling brotherhood, and teaching peace and community with all men."

"No God? No rules?"

"Well... we're still talking philosophy, which means using the story of Jesus to think about the story of our lives. The first insight we get from Jesus is that we need to change our consciousness. Once your consciousness shifts, you might also get the feeling that God comes with just one rule: Love."

Some years ago, my friend Josh Klein invited me down to his parents' place in the Caribbean to spend some time together and share our blossoming spiritual knowledge—yes, Josh's dad was "Mr. Klein" from other stories in this book.

One night, Josh and I were wandering along the beach wrapped up in talking about the idea of a loving creator and judgments on gender in Bible stories. The air was warm, and the moon was full; waves were lapping on the shore, and the sand under our bare feet was still hot from the day. The stars were blazing the way they do when there are no city lights.

And then something happened.

It was weird; it happened to both Josh and me at exactly the same time. A sense of belonging and forgiveness and love washed over both of us. It was as if the outer breeze moved something we both felt within our bodies. We felt both humble and powerful, and we were swept away by an insight, a sensation that we had hurt others and loved others and been hurt and could be healed. We both dropped to our knees. I remember I was crying, and then Josh was too. And we talked about how we both knew that through loving, we could be forgiven, because all humans fail. Lying on the beach, looking up at the stars, we felt that Jesus was walking with us and connecting to us, changing our consciousness. Maybe we didn't see an apparition, but we both felt the same overwhelming love for everything and everybody.

Time stood still.

We felt the Christ Consciousness. The feeling that was swirling in our souls held us, and kept us, so that ultimately we both changed our lives. In some way or another, since then, we've been trying to maintain that transcendent feeling as the center of our lives.

Josh gave up a multimillion-dollar trust fund and moved to a community dedicated to the teachings of the Cosmic Christ. That was over eighteen years ago, and he's still there. I was out there not long ago visiting him, his wife, and their four kids. They're happy people.

Unlike Josh, I chose to stay more in the mainstream (what Josh likes to call "the third dimension") and worship God while trying to maintain connections to the world in which I was raised and where I now make my way. Nevertheless, that ecstatic experience of being with Christ for those few minutes on that beach produced a hunger and a desire in both of us to connect our lives to that stream of Christ-conscious energy.

The most important thing I want to say about it is that we knew Christ was real. And maybe this is the critical distinction between a historical person called "Jesus" and the energy we experienced, which was inspired by the story of Jesus Christ.

The question with any Christ-and-consciousness problem is, was, and always will be, a biblical question: How are we to interpret the Bible? The main source we have for a model of Jesus is in the New Testament; but there are also the Dead Sea

19. What Do You Know About Jesus?

Scrolls and lots of papyrus rolls from Nag Hammadi called the Gnostic Gospels. For now let's stick with the version of the New Testament as decided by the Council of Nicea in AD 325. Using the same words from the Council of Nicea, different churches find different sets of rules for their churches and insist that the Bible, the New Testament in particular, means what they say it means. There are over 33,000 sects based on the teachings of Christ. I mention this simply to point out that even among "believers," there appears to be some major discrepancies as to what exactly are the "true teachings" of this Christ figure.

Jesus, like the Buddha, never wrote anything down himself, so everything has been remembered, recorded, translated, and then interpreted by the rule makers of a particular sect. Why are there so many different interpretations? The purpose of the differing interpretations of the rules is to keep each sect together and to distribute power within the sect. There are two problems facing any interpretation: the first is what makes a good person. The second is what makes a good sect. Reading the Bible only to find rules provides a whole lotta latitude for interpretation. So each sect—even if they're all versions of "Christianity"—settles on different emphases.

Many "Christian" sects, in their search for rules, insist that *every word of the Bible is true*: meaning all of the Old Testament as well as the New Testament is the revealed word of God and therefore indisputably true. For some Christians, this "indisputable word of God" concept can run into some contradictions in the modern world. There are quite definite Hebrew (Old Testament) laws against wearing cotton/wool blended clothing, eating shellfish, cutting your hair in a rounded fashion, and the dos and don'ts of gender-specific role-definition, and theses might seem silly to a contemporary Roman Catholic or Southern Baptist. Similarly, for many contemporary secular Jews those same strict laws of the ancient Hebrews seem unnecessary to the most central practice of their faith.

But there's also the problem with taking the "whole Bible" literally when, *in the Bible*, Jesus says that he doesn't agree with a lot of the Old Testament and says it *should be put aside*. For example, from the Gospel of Matthew: "You have heard that it has been said, An eye for an eye, and a tooth for a tooth. But I say to you, that you resist not evil: but whoever shall smite you on your right cheek, turn to him the other also." By saying that, Jesus was setting aside that part of Leviticus as false; turning the Old Testament rules of "an eye for an eye"—which justifies seeking revenge—into his New Testament's principle of love: instead of striking back, "turn the other cheek."

Jesus doesn't say this only about one verse in Leviticus, but in various Gospels, and the disciples all agree (which in itself is pretty unusual). In these passages Christ is setting aside a good portion of the Old Testament to offer an entirely new deal with God. At the Last Supper Jesus says that his blood, which is shed for all mankind, represents a "new covenant"—a new agreement between man and God. The old covenant was the Old Testament; the new covenant is "the Good News," and the "news" part is that you don't have to worry about the Old Testament's rules—you can wear a cotton and spandex t-shirt, enjoy clams casino, and have a bowl haircut and still love God. It's not about the rules! Jesus intentionally set aside "the letter of the law" because he wanted each of us to be ministers of the spirit. In 2 Corinthians 3:6 the apostle Paul says that Jesus "has made us able ministers of the New Testament; not of the letter, but of the spirit: for the letter kills, but the spirit gives life." The spirit is the sense of a principled feeling about life: don't fuss over rules—the letter

19. What Do You Know About Jesus?

of the law; instead, know your first principles—essentially a philosophical structure.

Rule-based religion, with its lists of rules that must be followed and if followed will make you a "good person," is a letter of the law structure. Obeying the rules without regard to each individual's feeling or rational judgment in a situation is what, in this approach, defines the moral life. But with the philosophical approach, instead of obsessing over lists of rules, we ask what is a "moral life" in the abstract—in the whole of life, is there a single principle, or at most, a couple of principles, that you can always use to interpret your best choices? Is a moral life following someone else's rules—the structure of religion—or is that just a reflex that prevents us from having to think for ourselves? Or does a truly moral life arise when individuals choose fundamental principles that they can apply flexibly? In fact, isn't that exactly why Jesus wanted to make a new covenant?

The question then becomes: Is there any point in the New Testament where Jesus says there are simple principles that will replace the Old Testament rules? Yep, both Matthew and Luke recall a conversation between Jesus and a wise and religious man. In the great Jewish tradition of discussing the Law, the man wanted to test Jesus' knowledge with a question about the Ten Commandments. "Teacher," the man asked, "which is the greatest commandment in the Law?"

By the way, this is a famous problem with the Ten Commandments and the subject of much debate: which of the ten should be most important? Is it more important to keep holy the Sabbath (which was Saturday, by the way), or not coveting your neighbor's ox (or wife)?

Jesus replied: Love the Lord your God with all your heart and with all your soul and with all your mind. This is the first and greatest commandment. And the second is similar: "Love your neighbor as yourself. All the Law and the Prophets hang on these two commandments." This was Jesus' way of revising the Ten Commandments 1.0 and updating them to Principles 2.0.

The wise old man, maybe a little miffed that eight commandments just got nixed, asked a tricky question. "Who is my neighbor?" And you can see that his implication is that "folks in my tribe or my sect are my neighbors, but everybody else, eye-for-an-eye, right?"

But Jesus wasn't down with that plan. He responded with the parable of the Good Samaritan. There was a Jew, he said, who had been attacked by robbers and was injured, maybe dying, by the side of the road. The Jew had been ignored by a rabbi and other Jews, but then a man from another tribe, a Samaritan, came by, and he stopped and tended to the injured Jew's wounds, put him on his donkey, took him to safety, and even paid for his hotel bill during recovery. Clearly, for Jesus, Jews and Samaritans are neighbors, and therefore all men and women are neighbors, deserving of the same devoted, selfless love we give to God who created us all. Two commandments, one love, and you have a bingo!

If you read the New Testament, you will see that Jesus' acts and teaching are sourced from love. He sees that all of us are created by God, and we best worship God by loving one another, and indeed, loving and caring for all God's creation. For Jesus, charity, fairness, optimism, and mutual respect—even that socialist idea about sharing limited resources equitably (i.e., the loaves and fishes)—are the ways we honor and love the Divine.

How did Jesus come by these ideas that made him the Christ?

To understand Christ Consciousness, you have to be a seeker. Jesus was a seeker, and like many of today's seekers, Jesus went back to nature; he went into the desert, into silence, for

19. What Do You Know About Jesus?

forty days, to better examine his faith, find God, and then find God in himself without the noise of people all around him. To understand Jesus' consciousness—to create in yourself Christ Consciousness—in your own mind turn down the noise of the crowd, your family, your relationships, other people's rules and expectations. Turn off your habits of comfort and beliefs about status. Instead, focus on three questions:

1) What is the nature of God?
2) How does God love us?
3) Can we love others the way God loves us?

That's what Jesus discovered in the desert.

As we consciously choose to look at the world through eyes of love and feel how God loves us, we start to understand that by nourishing and caring for our neighbors (Chinese, Palestinians, Nicaraguans, Sudanese, and so on), we're making more love—for others, but it will be reflected back to us as well. And by extension, when we care for the earth, which sustains our human neighborhood, we love all of God's creation. This is what Christ Consciousness is all about.

To feel Christ Consciousness, you don't need to call yourself a Christian or become a church member or follow the traditional religious rules. Instead, you find a way to constantly connect with the Divine, with the energy of other humans, with living things, and with the earth itself.

Jesus, like the Buddha, wasn't hung up on dogma. Both of them emphasized that right behavior was more important than rules, religious structures, idols, or rituals. If the church or the ritual assists you in living a more loving life, great. But beware of any group that puts their own tribal superiority as a purpose or rule. When Jesus says, "I am the way and the truth and the life. No one can get to the Father except through me," the "me" he was referring to was not himself as a physical being, but his "loving way" of being. He wasn't asking us to make him or his image into a holy idol; he wasn't setting himself apart for worship; he was asking us to look at what he did and see his life and teachings as examples of how to love deeper every day. It's his consciousness of love that constitutes "The Way."

For most of us, this requires a bit of change. Life tests our ability to see with Christ Consciousness, and it ain't easy. During your drive to work or while internet browsing or when you're on the job, are you activating love? Are these all acts of humor or joy or mercy? When you talk to your lover or a cashier or a policeman, how are you doing with openness, honesty, and forgiveness? Think about the Last Supper: Do you take the time to feel grateful for each meal, even that Snickers bar or that cuppa Starbucks? Gratitude is a portion of love. As you become principle-driven, you can expand your consciousness to see how compassionate God has been with you; pause, be grateful, then pass some of that along.

Like all births, to be reborn in your own Christ Consciousness will require some painful stretching. You may suffer a bit because, even if you observe how habitually fearful you are and see how unnecessary those fears are, they can still be very hard to give up. Therefore, you will have to unpack those fears and choose to replace them with love. Love yourself enough to take care of yourself, and some fears will immediately disappear. For some—and here's that painful stretching—you may have to change your work, your friends, possibly even your wasteful lifestyle. You will feel the danger of chaos when your comforts and rationalizations

19. What Do You Know About Jesus?

fall apart. But then the promise is to be reborn in love. In the story of the Resurrection, when Jesus is reborn, he has nothing left to fear; when you learn to live in Christ Consciousness, you too are released from fear: it's your own personal Second Coming.

As long as you're loving your neighbor and loving God, you're following Christ Consciousness and making the world a more peaceful place to be, whether you say you're a Christian or not.

Sweat This Out

Get the notebook out. Two days, two pages. Make a conscious choice to be kind to everyone. It doesn't matter who they are, and it doesn't matter how badly they screw up or even if they mistreat you. Put all of your focus on being present with them without fear or hatred and direct your heart to feel kind and forgiving. And then, as you say goodbye, try blessing them. Maybe even give a little bow of gratitude.

At the end of the day, number a list from one to five and give yourself credit for five kindnesses.

It's just two days. You can do this. How do you feel?

20. HOW OFTEN ARE YOU MOTIVATED BY GUILT?

I was walking out the door for school when my father stopped me with a command.

"Gregg, I need your car tomorrow."

"Dad, when the Klein's helped me to buy this car, they were helping me keep my job. You have a car."

"Gregg, I need to borrow your car tomorrow. You need to pitch in and do your part. Your car gets better gas mileage. And I can't afford another breakdown."

"I'm sorry your Buick gets crappy gas mileage. I'm sorry it breaks down, but that's not my problem. I need my car. You have your own."

"How can you be such a selfish, spoiled brat? Your father is going through a difficult time right now in his life, and you can't be there for him?"

"I don't think it's right of you to put the responsibility on me. I need my car to go to work to earn money to live. You seem to forget that 'my father' isn't giving me anything."

"Who do you think pays the rent? Who do you think buys the fuel?"

"Last Friday, we had no heat in the house, and it was below freezing."

"Gregg, don't be such a brat. I need your car tomorrow. I'll be

home by 3:30, you'll have your car back by the time you're home from school. You'll make it to work."
  "You promised that last week, and you didn't show until 6:30."
  "Give me the keys. I'm leaving now."
  "OK, I'm going to trust you to have it back. I can't be late to work. This is the last time I'm doing this, Dad."

My dad was a psychoanalyst, a PhD. He'd studied the way the human mind works, but the way he used this knowledge, I'd say he was a doctor of mind-fucking and guilt-tripping. He knew exactly what to say to make me feel guilty enough so I'd give him what he wanted. Usually, he wanted either my money or my car. The guilt worked on me. As I feared, he didn't show up on time, so I was late for work again. But it was the last time I let him engage me in the car conversation.

I think most of us feel the pinch of guilt from time to time and feel forced to do something we don't want to do, and then that sense of obligation overwhelms us.

It's a supremely useful perception to be able to separate a morally correct obligation from being manipulated by guilt, possibly even against your own best interest. Art Markman, PhD, writing in *Psychology Today*, offers this model for thinking about guilt:

> If you do something wrong that hurts someone else, you feel guilty. Guilt is a valuable emotion, because it helps to maintain your ties to the people in your community. It provides a painful consequence for actions that would weaken the groups that you belong to. Because guilt is painful, people often find ways to soothe their feelings by making up for their actions in some way. These repairs are

20. How Often Are You Motivated by Guilt?

also useful because they help re-strengthen people's ties to [each other and to] the community that they have damaged.

Markman is pointing out that if you or I do something that hurts another, we should feel guilt and an obligation to repair that hurt. It's up to each of us to be sensitive to those people we've hurt, but especially if someone actually tells us that we've hurt them, we need to make amends; in effect we're "mending" our relationship with that person. If we don't do that, then we've created a simmering resentment, and even other people who've observed the incident can be polluted with the bad feelings, and we can all become more fearful: collateral damage. If we do succeed at making amends, we can get multiple good results: we've given a benefit to another person, we've repaired trust bonds that may affect the community, and we have a refreshed consciousness of our responsibility.

But that's a healthy sense of guilt, not the game my father was playing. My father was implying that unless I made his needs more important than my own needs, I didn't love him.

Big difference—he was using "love" to manipulate me.

As he set it up, by depriving him of my car I was depriving him of love. And this is how the destructive side of guilt works: the circuit of actual responsibility gets rewired, so there is no sense of making amends for a specific problem; instead, both people are confused by unclear responsibilities.

The classic question of destructive guilt is: What obligations does "loving someone" incur?

In the case of dear old Dad, it was my car and I needed it, but he used father-son guilt to manipulate me by making me "responsible" for his transportation woes. He implied that in order for me to feel good about myself, I should let him use my car. I would be coming to the rescue, helping my father when he needed me. But it was only a convenience for him and a big inconvenience for me. In my heart, I resented the transaction. His love for me hadn't given me the car, nor was he even paying the heating bill like all the other fathers I knew. Worse, I didn't trust him to get it back to me on time. He had his own car, but like a two-year-old who sees another child's toy, he wanted mine because it was better. He'd done nothing to earn it; there was no upside for me except I could "take care of him."

Like me, many of us are manipulated by guilty reasons that somehow seem "appropriate" because they're based in a "love" relationship; we feel like we're taking care of someone who needs us. But we always need to ask: Is there an exchange of value or just manipulation by which one person loses value and the other gains?

In the healthy model of responsible guilt, if I do something that costs someone else materially or emotionally, I make up for it. I balance the scales. In the guilt-as-manipulation model, I do something that costs me; I gain nothing but credit for "love"; however, perhaps even unconsciously I will feel a powerful resentment later because I got a bad deal. Nevertheless, OK, I'll just suck it up because that other person couldn't take it. I nurture the illusion that I took care of someone I love, but I'm angry on some level because I didn't protect myself.

That simmering anger is destructive guilt. I allowed myself to be manipulated. And it gets worse: this can become a habit of mind. If your parent used this kind of "if you love me . . ." guilt manipulation when you were growing up, it can become a handle that others can use to control you.

Often this guilt transaction is expressed passive-aggressively: another person will subtly suggest that we "don't love them" unless we do their bidding; it could be a tone of voice, sulking

20. How Often Are You Motivated by Guilt?

behaviors, or other ways of withdrawing. We feel accused or blamed. We get the signal of their pain or need, so we think: Was this my fault? Should I feel bad? Do I need to compensate? The signals I'm getting say, "Yes! You should give me what I need," yet, in my sense of fairness, I don't feel like that "need" was my responsibility: I didn't create *their pain or need*.

Yet the overriding feeling is that I should make it up to this person because of the strength or clarity of their feelings. Because we're such sensitive social creatures, we're very alert to obligations and affections, so when someone willfully manipulates those signals, we can be vulnerable to neglecting our own best interests and sense of fairness. Each of us wants to be a good person, so if that's what I have to do . . .

My father claimed that if I loved him, I should lend him my car. But in the back of my mind, I knew that this was lopsided: a father's love shouldn't be contingent on taking his son's car (especially when his son is going to need it). Guilt works. My father had something I wanted—his love—so I'd do just about anything for it. He used guilt, and I went for it like a trout for a mayfly—a mayfly with a huge barbed hook in it.

We spend a lot of our lives hooked into and dragged around by guilt, but we don't *even know it* because we keep trying to taste that delicious mayfly of love. But there ain't no flavah in that damn feather lure. Yet dammit, it looked so delicious, like this time it was the real thing, this time I'll get love and respect. So we keep biting and not quite noticing.

Over time, instead of building a healthy balance of feelings and communication, mutual trust and respect—which is the mechanism of responsible guilt—we build up a pressurized mouthful of unexpressed emotions. When we don't feel our relationships are fairly balanced or honest, we become resentful.

If we don't express our resentments, they will build up inside of us as shame and frustration.

It can get so familiar that we start asking others to give us love or power that we don't deserve to compensate for our own feelings of impotence; we learn how to guilt-trip others.

Seeing and understanding destructive guilt—what is known as "the guilt trip"—is a key to adult responsibility and stability—maybe even happiness. To sort these feelings out, we need to tune in to our feelings of obligation or sacrifice. If we act out of a sense of obligation, it could be an appropriate and decent action, or it could be the result of manipulation. The trick is balance. If I get the kids at band practice, you make dinner. But if I'm getting the kids, making dinner, and working while you're on the couch watching Netflix and eating bonbons—Houston, we have a problem.

The emotion that would cause that kind of imbalance is fear. Understanding destructive guilt is tuning in to the fear that you will lose love. Destructive guilt looks backward and passively drifts into fear. If you have fantasies of getting back at or getting free of your manipulator, that's the best clue you have that you're being manipulated by bad guilt. When you have that festering sense of resentment, it's probably time to take responsibility for yourself. When you've done something out of a manipulated sense of obligation, the most important thing is that you don't keep doing it. In this, as in all things in life, if you find yourself thinking destructive or fearful thoughts about another person, you are responsible for changing that. But here's the hard part: the other person won't change, so you need to learn to refuse to be manipulated.

Refuse to be manipulated.

This will likely cause an explosion of emotions. Plan an exit. Don't go there. Walk away.

As it turned out, when I finally learned to deny my dad my

20. How Often Are You Motivated by Guilt?

car, I was doing the most loving thing I could: I was protecting myself and giving him fuller responsibility for himself. A key skill in loving another person is learning to resist guilty manipulation. Yes, sometimes we have an obligation that needs to be honored, but sometimes we're getting played—and we need to learn the difference.

Sweat This Out

The purpose of this exercise is to acknowledge the places where guilt could be sneaking in.

Part One: Recall yesterday: think of all the things you chose to do, particularly involving others, meetings, conversations, paying bills, giving rides, texting or making calls—any congress or commerce with other people.

How many actions did you come away feeling: "I got a benefit from that. I gave my time, energy, and attention, and I feel better; I feel like the other person got something good too." If that's how you feel, you can be pretty sure you had a responsible relationship.

Or did you avoid doing something just because someone asked you to? This is an anti-guilt reflex, and it can be as damaging as the guilt reflex. Sometimes we do owe people a consideration or a courtesy as part of relationship maintenance or because we've made an agreement with them. We need to honor those courtesies and agreements.

If, on the other hand, you felt bored or irritable, you were "doing a favor"; you were phoning it in for someone else's benefit. If you knew there were other things you wanted to do, other ways to spend your money or your time, but you had to do this other thing, that's guilt—obligation without enthusiasm.

Life is compromise, but there's a qualitative difference in emotional sense when we act out of responsibility and when we feel manipulated by guilt. We didn't make an agreement as much as knuckled under someone's else's convenience.

In your notebook, can you find something you did yesterday that you feel resentful for, something that was half-hearted or half-assed?

Whose purposes were you serving?

Part 2: Consider all the things you *thought* you were going to do yesterday. What has been left incomplete? The gym? Cleaning the house? Writing those emails? Paying bills? Checking your bank balance? Taking a walk in the woods? Getting in touch with that friend from high school who reached out to you? Meditating?

For all the things you didn't do, were you depriving yourself of a healthy thing—and what did you do instead to compensate for the negative emotions you generated by being manipulated? It costs us a certain kind of strength to give in to bad guilt. We become unable to do for ourselves and

20. How Often Are You Motivated by Guilt?

instead choose passive or destructive pleasure replacements such as watching TV, playing video games, excessive eating, and internet shopping for stuff we really don't need.

Notice that the sense of wasted time you have when you've substituted something "easy" for something that would have made you exercise self-control and thereby feel more powerful. You can catch yourself thinking it was just "easier" to watch TV, and you've found guilt. Often this kind of guilt is connected to rationalizing: By watching TV because it's "too hard" to get to the gym, the choice you're making is to rehearse powerlessness. And this creates regret that we feel powerless, so we choose passive or self-indulgent actions to compensate for the unpleasant feeling of powerlessness.

Powerlessness is learned: somewhere along the line, we learned that other people's feelings and needs—their power—was more important than ours: Mom or Dad, the priest, the teacher, or whoever taught you that their power was more important than yours by using shame, humiliation, or withholding love. Check yourself. Do you give in to unhealthy guilt? Is it connected to earlier relationships? If so, you're recreating your own powerlessness. It's up to you to walk away from the guilt and reclaim your power.

21. ARE YOU AN ADDICT? HOW LONG WOULD YOU STAY IN A RELATIONSHIP WITH AN ADDICT?

I was visiting my half-sister Louisa after she had gotten out of jail for the third time.
 "So what's the plan, sis?"
 "I'm figuring it out."
 "That's a good start."
 "Taking one day at a time."
 "Weeze, you're not drinking, are you?"
 "I couldn't drink in jail."
 "So that's a no?"
 "I didn't say that."
 "So you are drinking?"
 "I like drinking; it calms me."
 "Even with all the damage and destruction that it's caused in your life?"
 "I don't get shit-faced; I just keep it in my water bottle and take a sip when I want."
 "Wow, so drinking really is the most important thing in your life?"
 "Gregg, I don't want to talk about it anymore; it is what it is."

Is there a habit you have that is really engrained in your life?

27 QUESTIONS TO MAKE YOU SWEAT

Do you have to have a cup of coffee first thing in the morning? Do you salivate just thinking about dessert? Do you always speed on the highway? How about internet use? Shopping? Porno? YouTube and Instagram for hours at a time?

Here's the question: could you stop your habit now and not go back to it? Ever? Not that you have to, but could you?

My half-sister, Louisa, in the conversation above, confessed to being a hard-core, heads-up addict. She knew her drinking would kill her—and it did—and she kept drinking, but at least she was totally honest about it. Her honesty made it easier for me to love and forgive her even if I didn't want her drinking and would never help get her booze.

Addicts are difficult people. Their addictions sneak into their lives and the lives of those around them. It becomes easy to lie by omission about how addicted we are—and we'll talk about the ways we can be addicted in a minute—but addictions will hurt our relationships as much as sap our own individual power. So this chapter is a chance for you to see if you are addicted, how much you are addicted, and how your addiction may be affecting your relationships.

If you're addicted, that need is junk in your life. It could be sugar or shopping or heroin: it's all junk. My father's junk was alcohol. He was an alcoholic of the worst sort—the kind that clearly shows how the junk takes over.

When I was little, he was a practicing psychoanalyst, husband, homeowner, parent—you could say he was living the American Dream. Dad enjoyed a glass of wine or two with dinner, but he had made a good life doing difficult things, and a drink relaxed him. At a certain point, though, he had less and less money, and the wine became vodka.

Over time he became a different man; he did illegal things, he

21. Are You an Addict? How Long Would You Stay with an Addict?

lost his practice, he divorced my mom and more or less deserted his kids—me, my sister, and my brother. My father had become an addict. His addiction took over his life to the point where serving his addiction became the most time-consuming part of his life: getting alcohol, drinking alcohol, or dealing with the consequences of alcohol. Then, when he left his family, he was gone. Gone in the sense that he was never really a connective part of my life once he left when I was still a teenager. His emotions were invested in his addiction one way or another for the rest of his life.

The parts of life that demanded conscious responsibility were parts he simply ignored. Not a dumb guy, he went on to have some success managing a drug and alcohol rehab center; ironically enough, because he was still well-sauced as he did the job. Of course, eventually he crashed and burned, but for the rest of his life, he'd have periods of employment and even sobriety, yet they never lasted.

My father's transformation into a hard-core alky made a huge impression on me, so I've been careful in my life to take it easy on intoxicants, even though as a musician I'm in a world where intoxicants are easy to come by.

I don't know for sure if I have inherited the predilection for addiction, but if you define *addiction* as a "compulsive focus on a certain behavior, possibly to the detriment of the rest of life," I do fit the bill. I've gone through periods, even as a youngster, when I was obsessed with tennis or music. Much more than other kids my age, I was afraid that I wasn't doing it enough; I had a constant anxious feeling that I had to practice more. It got to the point where practicing tennis or music would take over my life. I could only see my days and even my relationships in terms of how they might affect my practicing. If I went a day without practice, I would find myself anxious, irritable, and unable to concentrate. I could see that my practicing might be beneficial to me as a player, but being obsessive about it was making me less sociable, less fun to be around, and "weird" to other people. I used practicing to replace relationships and avoid difficult responsibilities, and even if it was making me better at tennis or drumming, it was also making me constantly anxious. No matter what I was doing, I felt like *I should be practicing*.

I knew from my dad the destructive potential that comes with "obsessive fixation"—which is how I'm defining *addiction*. I'm lucky to have that knowledge, since it's made it that much easier for me to see my addictions and gradually get out of destructive habits and back to a more balanced life.

Let's hope addiction is an issue that you never have to face, but the numbers suggest you might. As of 2015, the statistics from the Substance Abuse and Mental Health Services Administration (SAMHSA), a branch of the US Department of Health and Human Services, found that 17 million adults in the U.S. suffer from alcohol abuse or dependence, and 7.5 million adults addicted to some form of drug use. That's 24.5 million people, or one in ten American adults, who are addicted to drugs or alcohol. But that's only substance abuse. Somewhere between 15 to 20 million adults and adolescents have pathological gambling addictions, and anywhere from 10 to 20 million (the statistics are obviously difficult to pin down on this one) Americans suffer from some form of sex addiction, including being addicted to pornography.

At this point, considering just those forms of destructive yet compulsive addictions, that's about one in eight Americans. And "Americans" includes children. So if we cut about 25 percent to allow for kids, that's about one in six of American adults. These figures get larger every year too; they actually grew about

21. Are You an Addict? How Long Would You Stay with an Addict?

345 percent from 2001 to 2016. The opioid epidemic alone is responsible for forty-six deaths a day—about 42,000 a year. Few of these people would have thought they were potential addicts before their first prescription.

So if you think that you couldn't be an addict, don't be so sure. Wait until your lower back goes kaflooey and your doc gives you a month of Percocet. Then we'll talk.

But we're just getting started with the human propensity for self-destructive obsessions.

Somewhere in the range of three million-plus Americans have some form of food addiction. These are people who eat (or don't eat), not for nourishment, but because eating is an anxious behavior. The obesity rate in the US is 39 percent for adults; obesity leads to type 2 diabetes, which is potentially fatal. Yet Americans consume massive amounts of sugar and fats in their sodas, candy, and junk food. By contrast, the obesity rate in Japan is 3.5 percent, where the government has established waistline limits that resulted in this remarkably low figure. (The Japanese government gives their overweight citizens up to six months to lose weight, and if they still don't meet the waist requirement, the government will impose financial penalties on companies and local municipalities with overweight people.) The Japanese rate of obesity is less than one tenth the rate in the US. Are the Japanese genetically less food-addictive, or do they understand that addictive behaviors can be—and perhaps need to be—communally recognized and addressed?

Addiction—in whatever form—works by changing your brain over time. In a non-addicted brain, natural inclinations and habits are regulated by natural cycles of bodily clocks and appetites. These natural regulators have evolved to sustain and protect us. This basic biology uses neurotransmitters to regulate our nervous system. Neurotransmitters tell us when we're hungry and signal when we're full. If we eat healthy foods, the desire to eat, and also the flavors and sensations of food, stimulate us so that we eat at the right times and the right amounts. We don't overeat because the flavors and sensations stimulate the right neuro-regulators. We know what kinds of food to crave and when to stop eating. However, eating foods made with simple carbohydrates (white bread, for instance) or sugary foods and drinking full glasses of sweet fluids while eating all can make it more difficult for our bodies to feel what we've just eaten. In addition, we feel hungrier sooner after a junk-food meal. Our body chemistry starts to crave sugar, which makes junk food or sugar addictions easy to acquire. Well, we don't want to call it an "addiction" exactly: everybody does it, it's convenient, it feels good, and the destructive effects aren't immediate. Everybody's got to eat, and it takes time to gain weight and create heart or hormone disease. After all, it's just a couple of Happy Meals a week, and our kids have been programmed to believe that processed, high-sugar factory foods are "good":

"We're going to McDonald's!"

"Yaaaaay!"

Adults eating conveniently will get just as hooked. And like all addictions, once you're hooked, you lose control and your reality (your brain) changes. On a chemical/neurotransmitter level, your bodies begin to crave only those foods.

To a junk-food junkie, cutting out all sugar and processed foods will feel unnatural and extremely uncomfortable. Even when they see that their health is suffering, they still may not change their habits, because of the way sugar withdrawal feels.

The point about addiction—whether food, drugs, alcohol, or

21. Are You an Addict? How Long Would You Stay with an Addict?

porn—is that brain chemistry changes the actual thoughts you think about yourself. Habit replaces choice. It doesn't matter if the habit is a croissant, heroin, gambling, porno, or shopping, your brain chemistry tells you that you have no choice.

If your life includes a range of healthy activities, that would suggest your brain chemistry is in balance. The difference is in the ability to make choices. A healthy brain can choose to turn off Facebook, but the addict—whose brain structure has been changed by the habit—can't choose when to use. And this is the fundamental problem of addiction. The addict's brain chemistry becomes altered to the point where the addict *believes that the addiction is the most important thing in life.*

Some brains are genetically more predisposed to make these changes than others, but every brain is capable of addiction. And under the wrong circumstances, we can all learn to be addicts.

Addiction has other dimensions. Even useful or benign behaviors can develop an addictive dimension. For example, perhaps you know someone who can't be separated from their phone. They literally can't go into a different room without it. This particular symptom is a new and very real psychological disorder—and it's happening all over the world since the advent of the smartphone. Phone addiction is part of the Millennial generation. It begins by relying on the phone at an early age for entertainment and communications. The "early age" part correlates to the "security blanket" phase of life. For previous generations, a security blanket or a certain toy became a reliable companion that comforted our fears; but we usually gave it up around age six or seven.

In 2017, according to the National Consumers League, 56 percent of all American children between the ages of eight to twelve have smartphones. At the age when healthy children were putting aside security blankets, these kids were getting a different sort of "blanket." These security blankets were inanimate, but they were soft and easy to keep close; we felt just a little more secure with them. Yet at a certain age, our minds grew up enough to learn we didn't need them.

Getting a phone before ten gives a still unformed child a semi-animate, powerful tool that changes their brain chemistry. For some children, their reliable and constant-companion phone feels safer to play with than directly interacting with other children or, God forbid, adults. In short order, the phone-addicted child will use their phone for tens of thousands of operations in a month. They will shy away from real people and can become fearful of traveling or entering any new place. Their brains have been changed by repeated behaviors, and their phone has impeded their natural ability to socialize with real people. Humans are social creatures, and we're designed to be with one another. Giving young children smartphones may interrupt the natural development of social skills and replace it with an addiction.

This is an addiction worth noting, not just as a warning to parents, but because almost any "good" thing, even useful technology, may have an addictive and destructive aspect.

If you have a behavior that's a habit you go to automatically, chances are good that it's an addiction. Addictions are all the same brain chemistry, which is a loop of desire connected to things that can hurt us over time. You can see this is a tricky business. Drugs, booze, sex, internet shopping, food, gambling, phone—perhaps you can honestly say that you never do any of these things in an addictive way. But . . . the chances are very good that you know someone who does. Be careful, because whether it's bread or heroin, Facebook or gambling, there are no

21. Are You an Addict? How Long Would You Stay with an Addict?

benign addictions. An addiction means our brain has become a slave to an external force. The addict has lost the ability to know what's in her or his best interests.

If you are addicted, getting un-addicted will require changing your brain, and that will likely be a painful process.

And now for the second part of the question: how long would you stay in a relationship with an addict?

> It wasn't even daylight when the phone cut my dreaming short. I was glad at least that my college roommate was with his girlfriend so he wouldn't bitch at me about the call.
> "Dad, why are you calling me at six in the morning?"
> "I need your car. You need to come pick me up at my home by seven."
> "What are you talking about—you live forty-five minutes away?"
> "Gregory, I'm not fooling around. You need to be here at seven."
> "Wait a minute, Dad, you don't get to call me at six in the morning and expect me to drop whatever is going on in my life to help you."
> "Gregg, this is very important. You need to be here at seven o'clock. Get off the phone so you can be here on time. Please, get up here. I'll see you in an hour."
> "Dad..."
> "Just get up here."
>
> Later that morning:
> "Thank you, Gregg. I'll see you later."
> "Dad, you need to be here no later than 2:30."
> "I'll be here."

27 QUESTIONS TO MAKE YOU SWEAT

"I'm telling you that you need to be here no later than 2:30. I have to be at work at 3:00. You have to be here no later than 2:30."

2:45 that same afternoon:
"Dad, what the hell?"
"Gregg, you can drop me in Armonk."
"What?"
"You can drop me in Armonk."
"No.
"What did you say?"
"I said 'No,' I'm not dropping you in Armonk. I'm late for work, and I need this job. I'm not dropping you anywhere. This is it. Once again, it's always your life that's more important; you don't care when you fuck up my life. But this is the last time this will happen because I am so entirely over dealing with you ever again."
"Gregory, you're taking me to Armonk."
"I wish you luck with your life that sadly will not include a ride to Armonk and no longer includes relating to your firstborn son."
"Gregory. You are going to take me to Armonk."
"No, I'm really not. I'm done. Don't call me again."

This question is one of the more supremely difficult ones in this book. It requires that you know you know—and probably think you love—an addict. Is your husband obese? Is your fiancé anorexic? Is your dad an alcoholic? Does your brother play video games for twelve hours a day? Does little sis have an unnatural attachment to her iPhone?

Let's say you do identify an addiction: How bad is it? How is the addicted behavior affecting you and your relationship with

21. Are You an Addict? How Long Would You Stay with an Addict?

the addict? And here's the key: To what degree are you personally complicit with the addiction?

Relationships are corrupted by addiction so that both the addict and those who care about him or her are in a cycle of mutual destruction—the addict's whole life may be destroyed, but those around the addictive behavior are drawn into the toxicity so they make moral compromises and suffer emotional—and possibly financial—losses. Contemporary psychology calls this "codependency." In a codependent relationship, friends become addicted to helping the addict, so the addiction has control of everyone. The mutual reinforcement keeps the cycle going. The addict fails; friends and lovers forgive. Rinse. Repeat. It's not about the reality, which is that the addict is slowly dying and is toxic to everyone. It's about the fantasy, which is that the addict is being saved. The addict is afraid to be without the fix; and enablers are afraid the addict will die if they don't take care of him. But everyone's life is centered on the addiction; they feel trapped in the Sphere of Fear.

In the Circle of Love, you have to have the strength to see the responsibility everyone involved has for the damage; in the Circle of Love, relationships are about reality. The reality is that we need to love ourselves enough to prevent the addiction from controlling our lives even when it's controlling the addict.

The lie we will tell ourselves is that the addict will die without us. The truth is that addiction is a cycle of behaviors, and we don't have to participate.

My dad's addiction was bigger than just drinking. The drinking wasn't always visible. He wasn't always shit-faced and incapable of carrying on a conversation. But in the first few years, as he became addicted, every part of his life and every person in his life became poisoned by the changes in his behavior—the lying, the self-deceit, the dishonest dealings with both money and in his profession—it was all because alcohol was becoming his first choice for everything.

Most importantly, he saw it. He would admit that his need for a drink was controlling him—after all, he was a psychotherapist—but he didn't even try to stop drinking; he believed he was still doing "the right things that needed to be done" and that he was in control of when he drank. Dad's addiction was a bloodsucking vampire, sucking the blood not just out of him, but out of all of us. The morning he tried to manipulate me one more time into giving him a ride was the moment I realized that I'd been down that road too many times before and I had to get myself out of the cycle if I was going to have any shot at getting my life together. Dad and I would have to part. That day I washed my hands of any future codependent bullshit.

When someone relies on you to keep them afloat while they are actively abusing a substance, and you see their life is in a downward spiral because they are controlled by addiction, you are in danger of being sucked into the spiral of misery. If they don't stop using or if you can't figure out a way to extricate yourself from the relationship, their need for a fix will translate into their need for you: as a result, your best intentions, things you do that feel like love, are really just helping to stick the needle in, buy the booze, open the door to the toilet for the bulimic to vomit. The danger is that by trying to help while they are abusing, you signal that you're supporting the abuse *no matter what you might say*. You are an agent of that slow suicide.

Maybe I was lucky with my dad in that his addiction was so obvious. He would put things in terms of father/son relationships and play on my guilt, but I could see the drinking and the effects of the drinking, and I finally saw clearly that as long as he kept

21. Are You an Addict? How Long Would You Stay with an Addict?

abusing alcohol, he'd be abusing me. I couldn't help him stop drinking; I could only help him get to the next drink. I was always compromising my time, my car, my feelings about love. Getting my father out of my life would not only free me from his addiction and a nagging feeling of moral compromise—it was my only hope to recover my own self-esteem.

My father is (if he's still alive) an alcoholic. Even when he stopped drinking, he was controlled by alcohol. And he did stop around twenty years ago; he'd moved to California to get a "fresh start." He seemed to really change. He checked himself into a rehab center to dry out. He thought he replaced drinking with what he called the "sober life." He'd call and talk about how his relationship with God gave him strength to stay sober. He was high on God, which always struck me as strange for a man who had been a fervent die-hard atheist most of his life. He went so far as to admit all the mistakes he'd made; he swore he wanted to make amends so he could have a loving relationship with his children again. *Great,* I thought, *I've got my dad back!*

In our phone conversations, he talked about coming back to visit, getting right with his family, but it stayed at the level of phone conversations, and that "spiritual" talk only lasted a year or so until he wasn't talking about God anymore. Around that time, my uncle and my cousins—who saw him frequently—told me that he was back to cradling a jug of Gallo Hearty Burgundy with him at all times. The bottle had a permanent seat next to him in the car. Gallo had replaced God as his copilot. Back in the saddle again, out where a drink was his friend. At a certain point, we were on the phone, and I had to ask if he was drinking again. He hung up on me. I still made the effort for several years, but we never got past the first minute on the phone. He loved the booze more than me . . . more than anything.

Roger that, Pops.

Addiction is a monster. Monsters devour everything within reach. If you're close to a monster, you have to ask, can a monster ever be tamed? The answer is no. The monster has to tame itself.

Real love starts with responsibility. Your first responsibility is to yourself, and that is to tell the truth to yourself—and ideally to the addict as well. If you find yourself in the room with a monster, you and the monster need to agree that the monster is there. You can't kid yourself that it's just Dad in a drunk costume. No. Dad is being devoured by the monster—and the monster is also coming for you. When you are fully responsible for protecting yourself, you give the addict the full responsibility for their addiction—which up until then, you have been co-dependently supporting. You have to get out of the monster's room. When the monster is alone, she or he will see more clearly. The most difficult aspect is that, to recover from addiction, the addict must first admit that he or she has a problem, and only the addict can decide they want help to permanently remove the junk, the booze, the habit, the internet porn, the addictive destroyer from their lives. When the addict tames the monster, then there's a possibility for relationship. But only when the addict is no longer using.

The research on addiction is clear. If an addict is going to come to sobriety and healing, the sooner those around him refuse to support the addiction, the better. Psychologists recommend that, whenever possible, allow for only a very short tolerance period because showing the addict a hard boundary between his addiction and his family and friends will be a clear lesson in consequences before the addiction has had time to take hold: "You have a choice; your dope/booze/porn/etc. or your loved ones." At the same time, family and friends must be steadfast, not lured into new habits of trying to "help" before the addict is

21. Are You an Addict? How Long Would You Stay with an Addict?

fully sober. "Helping" will turn into a signal to the addict that "just a little bit of addiction" is somehow OK. And perhaps more importantly, family and friends must be on guard to protect their own mental and financial health.

But it's much easier said than done.

To shut out your child or parent or sibling, your boyfriend or girlfriend—to stop what you think is a love relationship—is a hardship unlike any other choice we might make in life. It requires tremendous emotional strength. For any of us to make that radical choice about a loved one who has a habit, you must be clear about how powerful addiction is; that for the addict, in their soul, the addiction feels more important than anything in their life. Once an addict has given in to the deadly power of their need, they are permanently changed, and those around them need to permanently change as well. The poison is contagious. You can't kid yourself that the person you knew is just a week in rehab away.

Yes, it seems wrong somehow to walk away from a person who is sick and unable to stop destroying himself. We want to help. We can read countless books on the subject, we can attend countless hours of therapy, we can watch countless documentaries on addiction, but until the addict in our life realizes that they are addicts and they want help to become un-addicted, even though we might tell ourselves we're loving them by standing by them, our support is just encouraging and enabling the addiction.

If you are currently confronting this problem, you shouldn't try to go it alone. You will need to recruit friends and allies to support you in protecting yourself, and you will need to educate yourself.

Remember first and foremost that by helping the addict in any way besides naming the monster, you're actually helping the addiction. By protecting yourself and getting away from the addiction and the addict, you're not abandoning the addict; you're empowering the addict to see clearly without the interference of your "good" intentions. The addict alone must decide that they want to change before any true healing begins. If you are not the addict, the only choice you have is to protect yourself from the addiction.

Find out about your local AA (alcoholics anonymous), GA (gamblers anonymous), DAA (drug addicts anonymous), SAA (sex addicts anonymous), OA (overeaters anonymous). AL-ANON is an organization to support those who are trying to break their co-dependency with an addict. If someone you love should lose themselves in addiction, read up on the latest treatment therapies, seek out professional help, and find out what you can do to help yourself stay sane.

Sweat This Out

Get out the notebook; write down your habits. Good? Bad? Middling? What do you do regularly? You should include all regular, repeated behaviors. Going to work or to class; cooking or shopping; video games or other forms of self-pleasure, yes, masturbation; include bedtimes and going to the gym. Regular, repeating behaviors. Make a nice long list. Not addictions, just habits.

Now on another page: who do you know that might be an addict?

Don't worry about how severe the addiction is,

21. Are You an Addict? How Long Would You Stay with an Addict?

but what behaviors do you observe that control the person rather than the person controlling the behavior? It's likely that these will be more public parts of our friends and family, but you can notice addiction in many socially acceptable habits. Sports fans can be controlled by their fandom, for instance. Politics can be addicting. Food. Work. Aggressive driving. Look hard. Observe other people's habits.

Now: review both lists and think . . . without making a judgment about good or bad: Are you an addict? Where are your addictions? Sugar? The Oakland Raiders? Online shoe shopping? Grannyporn?

What habit has you and controls you versus you occasionally doing that thing?

What are you doing to a potentially destructive level?

If you know someone that you think is an addict, can you ask them about the truth of their behavior?

22. HOW IMPORTANT IS IT TO POLICE LANGUAGE USE?

There was a stack of books left on a table after the lecture, and I was in charge of the cleanup. The other man of the two-person crew was Tom.

Tom asked me, "Did you see who left the books?"

"I think it was the gay guy."

"You can't say that."

"Can't say what?"

"'Gay guy.' It's prejudiced."

"Huh?"

"It's totally offensive."

"To whom?"

"To all the gay people in the world."

"You're not gay. I'm not gay. Who got offended?"

"Your prejudiced behavior is offensive to me. I'm speaking for gay people."

"Isn't it a bit presumptuous for a straight, white man to speak for all the gay people in the world?"

"It's not right to discriminate and disparage a whole group of people in society."

"I didn't disparage anyone."

"Yes, you did by calling him 'gay.' You singled him out with a pejorative."

"Gay people call themselves 'gay.' I didn't hurt him, and I'm not insulting gay people."

"Yes, you're doing all of those things when you make his gender preference the only way you identify him."

"I was just saying it so you knew who I was talking about in that crowd of thirty dudes. He was the gay guy, and he was cool with looking gay."

"It's just insensitive."

"Whoa, I thought I was just answering your question in a way you'd understand. You're the one who's judging him by his gender preference. It's making you uncomfortable. Not him. Not me. Would it be better to have said 'That homosexual man in the purple sweater and rainbow scarf?'"

"Why is his sexuality relevant? You could have just said the guy with the purple sweater and rainbow scarf."

"Yeah? But why was he wearing the rainbow scarf? It makes a statement, don't you think? What if he had no hair and I said, 'The bald guy.' Would that be offensive?"

"If a bald person would be offended by being characterized that way, then, yes."

"But how do you know what offends anyone? Are you the word police? Oh sorry, officer, scratch 'The gay guy.' Perhaps I should've said, 'That handsome fellow with all the product in his abundant hair and the flashy rainbow scarf?"

"That would be an option."

"But you knew who I meant with fewer bullshit words when I said, 'The gay guy.' What's your beef? You're not gay. Why are you offended?"

In that conversation, to my mind, I was being open and honest, and trying to find the owner of the books. I didn't think

22. How Important Is It to Police Language Use?

I was being prejudiced. Tom apparently had some experience that taught him that straight men should never refer to gay men as gay. And he put himself in the unusual position of being offended on behalf of all gay people and accusing me of prejudice—when, in fact, I believe in gay rights, and I have gay friends. But Tom is not the only person that feels that he should take this responsibility on himself.

The Oxford English Dictionary defines *political correctness* as "the avoidance of forms of expression that are perceived to exclude, marginalize, or insult groups of people who are socially disadvantaged."

Let's look at the problem of words as the dictionary addresses it. This dictionary definition emphasizes the fear aspect of what we say: be wary of what words you use because words might suggest an insult or a prejudice. In brief, don't say certain words for fear that someone else may feel discriminated against or demeaned.

On the one hand, this is reasonable—even sensitive. Certain pejoratives have been used as curses in the past; a person, once labeled as [insert your pejorative of choice here] could be prevented equal treatment under the law, and the use of that word might be a preamble to violence. Certain kinds of words are tied to immoral acts. As good citizens we don't want to bring back slavery, or encourage antisemitism, sexism, homophobia, or mob violence, and therefore it doesn't make sense to use language that, in context, has the force to support and nourish these terrible things.

Dr. Martin Luther King's famous insight about equality was: "No one is free until we're all free." You can't have a functioning democracy if some people are "more free" than others, and the ones with more freedom try to use language as a weapon to intimidate others. That's the moral problem of the historical weight of certain words. They might prove powerful enough to deprive a person or a group of a sense of freedom and equality—or even their actual relative freedom and equality.

But freedom cuts both ways when it comes to language. The first amendment in the Bill of Rights to the U.S. Constitution enumerated guaranteed freedoms: "Congress shall make no law . . . abridging the freedom of speech, or of the press."

And in the footnote: "Congress shall make no law respecting an establishment of religion, or prohibiting the free exercise thereof; or abridging the freedom of speech, or of the press; or the right of the people peaceably to assemble, and to petition the Government for a redress of grievances."

This is the guarantee of freedom of speech in the constitution, and herein lies the conundrum: If Congress can't "abridge the freedom of speech," then why do certain groups think they can make themselves language policemen? Language police exist on both sides of the political divide.

At the extremes, both conservatives and liberals want to control some words—Christmas, multiculturalism, sassy, nappy-headed, Nazi, thug, abortion—and try to enforce what they've decided are "acceptable limits" on speech—as if speech were a speed on the highway.

This attitude assumes that people must be protected from speech, but the Constitution insists that citizens must be at liberty to speak freely. This right to speak freely actually *is not freedom to say whatever you want*. There are limits to free speech—the limit is that speech is free until you're saying something that would cause harm to another person. The classic example is that we are prohibited from yelling "Fire" in a crowded theater unless there is a dangerous fire menacing the crowd.

22. How Important Is It to Police Language Use?

Speech correctness in some ways boils down to the classic playground problem: "Sticks and stones may break my bones, but words will never hurt me" unless the words could actually lead to sticks and stones. "Never" must be taken with a grain of salt. But let's not forget the "playground" part: ultimately, if we're playing with one another, we should be friendly and playful. But if we're hurting someone else, we're no longer on the playground, we're on the battlefield.

The insistence on "speech correctness" means that certain rules about "correct" speech pertain in all situations. Under these circumstances there is no playground for language, only the battlefield. On the battlefield of extreme speech policing, the fear of "oppressive language" means that some words, attitudes, and actions are always incorrect, and only The Enemy will use them. "Happy Holidays" . . . or is it "Merry Christmas?" Who is The Enemy? In the sixties nobody on television ever said "Crap," and now you can hear it on the evening news. Up until the 2000s the word "pussy" was reserved for rude men in locker rooms, but now that's changed. It's a kind of fundamentalism dividing the world into those who use language "correctly"—the saved—and those blasphemers who dare to use words in less regulated ways—the damned.

Let's call a truce on the battlefield for just a moment and do something completely crazy—let's define our terms.

What is a word?

A word is a placeholder for an idea. We use words to show each other what our ideas are.

If I say the word *car*, it's not about material reality. I haven't just given myself a car by saying the word. But I have a placeholder that will refer to any automobile I want to point at. To my Toyota Corolla or your Mercedes S Class or the flippin' jalopy that nearly hit my dog. They're all cars, and the word unifies a category of thought.

Words may conjure different emotions or different thoughts, but those are interpretations of the listener. Tom couldn't know my attitude about homosexuality when I used the word *gay*, just like you can't know how I feel about a certain German car just because I use the word *Mercedes*. Yes, *Mercedes* is much more specific than *car*, but it has in itself no more than the identification of that brand; it's not necessarily connected to emotion. But with other words—and especially with action words—you do understand how I feel about "the flippin' jalopy that nearly hit my dog."

The words themselves are not reality. When they are used to curse, accuse, humiliate, or manipulate, they gain an emotional traction that is not part of their original basic meaning. When words take on these potentially violent dimensions, the playground is transformed into the battlefield.

The words in the abstract are neutral, even arbitrary. Why do we call a car a car when we English speakers all agree that cars are automobiles? In other languages, *car*, or words that sound like car, mean different things. Words themselves are just arbitrary representations of categories, persons, places, actions, things, and other particles of language. The worst curse you can imagine in English means absolutely nothing to someone who speaks only Swahili. However, some people insist that certain words have specific denotations and connotations. *Denotation* is the dictionary definition: "the most objective sense of the word." *Connotations* are connections to personal, historical, and cultural realms.

On the language battlefield, there are language police—on both sides of the political fence—that insist that certain words

22. How Important Is It to Police Language Use?

come with specific connotations. You will recognize these two contemporary examples of language policing: the "N-word" and the "F- bomb." These are the only way we can "correctly" express two words that have troubled connotative history. However, perhaps you've noticed that even if you say N-word or F-bomb, in your mind—and the listener as well—are still thinking the actual word that's banned. But by saying the appropriate version, you politely avoid offending the language police—but everyone knows the words you're talking about.

Here's where it gets weird. When is the use of a dangerous word the equivalent of yelling "Fire!" in a crowded theatre? Should we permit kids in school to read *Huckleberry Finn* with the words Mark Twain wrote left intact, or should we ban the book for its poisonous content? Or perhaps we should print new versions and replace Twain's uses of "nigger" with "N-word." Twain meant for Huckleberry Finn to expose the evils of racism. The love between Huck, a white boy, and Jim, a black man, is the point of the book. Despite all the N-words, love is what matters.

We need to be able to judge the difference between historical context and malice, between discussion and oppression, between well-intended humor and vitriol.

Another form of language-policing is the "trigger warning." The trigger warning is presented to students before they read or see certain books or movies. They're warned that there may be upsetting content that might trigger upsetting emotions. This is a form of soft censorship. Once again there is a policeman who has prejudged the effect of language. It's like putting yellow tape around a crime scene because there's blood on the ground. But this yellow tape is strung around books or movies, sometimes classic works that generations of Americans have safely read or watched (such as *Huckleberry Finn*).

27 QUESTIONS TO MAKE YOU SWEAT

A book or movie is not the same thing as a crime or a crime scene. Instead it's an exercise for the imagination. If it is upsetting, that's part of its force, its value, its beauty. Othello suffocates Desdemona. Bob Ewell, the town drunk, describes his daughter's rape in *To Kill a Mockingbird*. The boys kill Piggy in *Lord of the Flies*. All of these are upsetting events, as well they should be. None of it is actually real. These are imaginative works of fiction intended to illuminate difficult ideas and render the problems of history, race, gender or culture understandable.

But in preventing the student from ever being "triggered," what else is prevented? The trigger warning is in an educational context; but is it educational to pretend that disturbing or unpleasant things don't happen in the world? Isn't education supposed to prepare us for what *does* happen in the world? And might it not be wise to reveal the terrifying range of human behaviors through words—abstractions and fictions in a controlled educational environment—rather than use that environment to keep students comfortable and entirely unstressed? Isn't the purpose of education to prepare our minds to better cope with such things when the reality presents itself? If I read about rape or racism, yes, it was really upsetting for fourteen-year-old me, but I learned to think morally in the fictional context which prepared me for later experiences; I was empowered by going through the upset. Learning to recognize immoral acts strengthened my moral core.

Schools, where well-educated teachers are trained to bring new ideas to young brains, are ideally intended to present socially redeeming texts to expand the limits of students' understanding. Trigger warnings have the potential for both limiting what teachers can use to provoke and inspire students and creating students who are left more ignorant about the ways of a diverse, competitive, and often disturbing world. The language police

22. How Important Is It to Police Language Use?

must be aware of the importance of emotional education and the difference between reading and reality.

The First Amendment is law: it's part of the basis of our nation; we must be able to have free and open discussions of opinions without shouting "Fire!" in a crowded theater. But language-policing has taken the form of law in some academic and social contexts; it's become like a religious dogma whereby correct formulas are decreed by a dominant interest. And yet the purpose of language is to communicate ideas between people so meanings can be negotiated; that's called understanding. Trigger warnings and dogmatic meanings can be a set of inflexible rules determined by cultural interests in order to preserve their institutional power instead of liberating speakers and listeners to work things out.

Language police can lead to thought police, and that's the whole problem of language where words are symbols and there the meanings are held in our heads. When you start to police usages then you have thought police. Thought police are the way authoritarian regimes intimidate and control whole populations. It's a fear-based technique: we should be afraid to use certain words because we're afraid to offend certain people who might be afraid to tell us how they feel about the language we use. Yikes!

And now I'd like to bring it back to the most essential question: What about love? Can we examine how language use can generate more love instead of more fear? Love isn't simply protecting—it's helping your loved ones to develop a deeper understanding, a more varied appreciation for complexity and beauty, for the way that each of us is human, and for how our human feelings are connected to the language we use and the images we envision. Love builds courage and insists on understanding. One of the great values of literature is in building empathy, but it comes from literary works that disturb us.

27 QUESTIONS TO MAKE YOU SWEAT

Regarding wisdom, self-esteem, and experience, not everybody has those qualities in equal measure. But no one has ever become wise or had their self-esteem strengthened by pillow fights. Fear puts pillows on things that don't need pillows: words, books, movies—these media are created to touch us emotionally, perhaps even to upset us, but they do it in the abstract. We can think about these things, which may be upsetting, and still be strengthened by them. Wisdom comes from thinking challenging thoughts and then applying them to the real world.

To ensure a civil society, it's proper to teach that hate speech is wrong because of its history—the fact that it's often been used to incite violence. And at its heart, its intent is to hurt, humiliate, and marginalize. Part of hate speech is the context and the tone that is used. Calling someone gay to their face could be used as a threat, but in another context, as in my example, it was used as a realistic descriptor: I wanted the gay guy to get his books back; there was goodness in my heart. Compare my example to marchers carrying torches and chanting, "Jews will not replace us!" and "White Power!" I think the difference is clear.

One of the best English classes I ever had was one when the teacher invited us to write every "bad word" we knew on the board and then, as a class, read them out loud, together. It was hilarious. And we all felt unified yet freer by doing it. No one was damaged by "nigger" or "no-dance-white-boy," or "asshole" or "cunt" or "kike" or "hillbilly" or "Polock" or "shithead" or "fuckface." We got to see the words in the light of day and in the context of the classroom. The fact that I learned something from it is obvious because of what I've just written. And everyone in the class loved everyone else just a little more for having taken this linguistic leap of faith together. Freedom—real freedom—is also love.

22. How Important Is It to Police Language Use?

How do we talk respectfully to one another? The only way to know if words are actually being used violently is to prolong the conversation. This requires equal parts bravery and compassion. Unfortunately there is no rule that makes certain words wrong every time. A key idea is that people who disagree with us are still people, not villains. We should both learn to say and learn to hear: "I felt insulted by that remark. Did you mean to hurt me with your words?"

But we get nowhere if we either act out of prejudice (having pre-decided that anyone using the "wrong word" is a bad person) or out of fear (running screaming from the room afraid of being triggered). What is more important in a democracy than standing up for your beliefs, and learning how to defend those beliefs through the powerful art of debate and/or discussion based on critical thinking?

Critical thinking is an often-misunderstood term that's become a cliché in high school and college, but what does it really mean? It means being able to distinguish between a word, an idea, and an action, and recognize the difference. It means being able to recognize a fact and differentiate between an uncomfortable fact and a comfortable belief. If someone insults me and I tell them that their words hurt me and then ask them why they are trying to hurt me, I become an uncomfortable fact in the face of their comfortable belief. But I have to love myself enough to have that courage, and I have to love my neighbor enough to trust he will understand me.

What if we put down the phones and the websites and the guns and took the time to talk to and listen to one another?

27 QUESTIONS TO MAKE YOU SWEAT

Sweat This Out

Listen for speech that offends you. Get out your notebook and write down exactly what is said that offends you. Just turn on cable news: Fox or MSNBC or CNN, Rush Limbaugh—or pick up a copy of the *Wall Street Journal* or the *New York Times*. Notice your emotional reactions. Rage. Joy. Fear. Surprise. Schadenfreude (look it up!). Write a lot. Let yourself open up and feel those harsh connections.

Notice that these are just words.

23. WHAT PART DO YOU PLAY IN ECONOMIC JUSTICE?

A sense of justice is the grease that lubricates the social gears of democratic societies. Justice comes from a belief that *fairness* is not just possible but a priority in economic, social, and governmental relations. In democracies, fairness comes from one very simple idea: "all men (and women) are created equal." Therefore, we should all be protected equally by law, and we should all have fair and equal rights and opportunities. And therefore, we are all obliged to obey the law. However, to achieve this community of equals, each of us should be willing to take responsibility for the function of the social order. The theory is that the more *everyone* takes responsibility, the more responsive the democracy will be—and the more the citizens can trust in fairness for everyone.

One way we can see the equality of a social order is by looking at economic issues, at the way money works. *Economic* justice is a key piece of a democratic social order; economic justice happens when we see that fairness and equality apply over a range of issues, from wages and compensation to taxation, government services, and the relative value of the stuff we buy.

Mr. Klein thought he was having a bad day. We were getting a little extra exercise to help him blow off steam by walking the two hundred yards to his private tennis court instead of taking the golf cart. "I had to pay a forty-five million dollar fine to the Securities and Exchange Commission. Those government fuckers."

"Sounds like a lot of money, Mr. K."

"You have no idea how much money that is."

"Well, you could say that while I have no idea how I would personally spend that much money, I certainly have some idea of the buying power it represents. Forty-five million dollars is enough money for me and pretty much everyone I know to live the rest of our lives in total luxury."

"Forty-five million dollars is a lot of money to pay for a government fine, Gregg."

"Mr. K, c'mon, is it really that much money in relation to the billion dollars you have?"

"It's a hell of a lot of money to pay for a fine to the government."

"First, it's a fine; you did something wrong. But OK, Mr. Guilty-as-Charged, I know you don't want to discuss it, but be real for a minute. Let's say I lose forty-five dollars; my life won't change. That's about what forty-five million is to your billion. Is anything going to change in your life? For you, it's just pocket change that fell behind the sofa cushions. You're not even going to miss it. Will your electricity be shut off because the bill isn't paid? Are your kids going to have to take out loans to go to college?"

"I like how you can be so relaxed with my money."

"It's all relative, right?"

"Well, I guess at some level."

"But you do realize that you're actually above the level of relativity? It's really not relative to you the way it is to 99.999 percent of the rest of the world."

"Of course it is."

23. What Part Do You Play in Economic Justice?

"Of course it isn't. If I had a fistful of parking fines that I hadn't paid and they caught up with me, it could run me maybe thousands of dollars, and my life would change. My experience of being alive would go from my current sense of relative security to having to scrimp and save and even borrow a few bucks here and there just to get by. But here's the big difference between you and 99 percent of the rest of the world. Let's say you had to pay ten, no twenty, times that 45 million dollar fine—you'd have to cough up a cool nine hundred million dollars right now. That's almost a billion. Ouch! You'd be down to your last measly 100 million. Yes, that's most of your money gone, but 'relatively speaking,' nothing in your life would change one iota. You'd stay out of jail, you'd keep earning money at the same rate, and your daily routine, your family, and your wine cellar would all be the same. Your ego might be bruised but you'd still have more than ten times as much money as it would take for me and my closest friends and family to live in ridiculous luxury for the rest of our lives."

"You speak with such authority for someone who's never made any real money."

"The amount of money you have is not relative, Mr. K, and you know it. You and your rich friends love to say, "Oh, it's all just relative," so you can feel like you're only a little bit better off than the rest of us: 'relative' is just your way of rationalizing your wealth so you can feel like 'we're all in this life-thing together.' How 'real' is your money if you could lose most of it and never miss it?"

"You're right, Gregg. I completely agree with you. It's a dog-eat-dog world, and I'm the big dog. You should get over it."

"Remind me, what is it you do that deserves to be paid at such a humungous scale, far beyond so many other hardworking people?"

27 QUESTIONS TO MAKE YOU SWEAT

"I'm the big dog. You should get over it."
"So says Mr. Guilty-as-Charged."

In Mr. K's thinking, democracy doesn't matter. He contributes vast amounts of money to various politicians to make laws that enable him to make even more money, not so everyone has an equal chance. On the one hand, he thinks he's doing his democratic part by supporting political candidates. Yet the amount of money he throws around creates more economic injustice if those candidates then make laws so he can stay the "big dog."

The vast majority of Americans today agree that economic injustice is a problem, given that only a few "big dogs" have so much wealth and have control over both politics and the various ways money is earned and distributed. A sizable portion of the population has experienced a loss of economic power in a single generation and are all collectively asking: How can we get our economic justice back?

When you think about your part in "economic justice," what comes up?

Brief pause while you think this over . . .

"My part? I pay my taxes and buy stuff. That's about it."

OK, that's a starting point. But if we dig into this subject in depth, we will come to find the truth that economic justice is in a state of crisis, and something everyone can do is take the time to see what's really happening. We tend to get stuck on our own stuff and forget to look around at bigger trends.

The economy is a system composed of many parts, and each effects the smooth operation of the whole. Each of us needs to look beyond our immediate and personal concerns and see who benefits from the system and why. We need to consider

23. What Part Do You Play in Economic Justice?

what actions we can take to cause systemic change. Each of us has to apply a sense of fairness to thinking about choices and conversations we can have that can help turn the trend back to a more just society.

What is different today than back in the seventies is that today the richest 1 percent in the United States own more wealth than the total of the bottom 90 percent. Is that an indication of economic justice—or economic sickness?

Money is power—but the weird part is, money has value only because we agree to it. We use money as a tool to get power but also to assign value—obviously the value of goods and services, but also the value of people. For the vast majority of us, dollars really are relative. We agree that a hundred dollars represents a certain amount of power—call it energy—that will be a placeholder we use for exchange so we don't have to barter for everything.

Most of us earn our placeholder/dollars through work, exchanging our limited resources or time, effort, and talents for dollars that give us power. Our efforts are rewarded according to socially constructed values. Then, after we earn our placeholder/dollars, we can use them to pay for rent or groceries, hire services, pay taxes, or build an outhouse or a tower with our name on it. We believe some skills and contributions are worth more than others. For example, a carpenter should be worth X amount of dollars an hour; a teacher should be worth Y amount; a banker should be worth Z amount—and that "should" is a perception of level of skill and power of contribution. "Perception" is the key concept. How we perceive value in a profession or in a product is the key to what we think its dollar value is. The purpose of the section below is to show you how that belief system about value is currently working and offer insights into both how it came to be and how it might change to curve more toward justice.

27 QUESTIONS TO MAKE YOU SWEAT

Let's look at the numbers to see how We, the People, through our use of power/dollars, see fit to spend and to pay for various professions and the goods they create. But let's *also* look at how we have spent our votes to create laws, taxation, and representative government to slice the American economic pie.

What does the following data tell you about our current beliefs regarding economic justice?

Poverty.

Poverty is a term used by the government to determine eligibility for aid based on income. The poorest Americans are a family of four who earn $25,000 or below; they qualify for maximum government support. However, government aid in benefits can extend to an income as high as $100,000 for a family of four, most of which are healthcare and insurance benefits. In the U.S., about 40 million people live at or below that bottom poverty-income level. Some are people with full-time jobs, but others are people with disabilities, on unemployment insurance, or without any income for whatever reason. More than one in ten Americans, many of them children, still live in poverty.

When it comes to getting exact numbers on income averages in the U.S., the numbers fluctuate a bit, depending where you're getting the information. According to the Bureau of Labor Statistics (BLS), the average wage for workers in 2019 was $47, 060, or about $905 a week. But according to the U.S. Census Bureau, the median household income stands at about $61,372 per year, or $1,200 a week. The major differences are that BLS collects actual data on individual wage information, while the Census Bureau conducts surveys and estimates household incomes.

Here are some more numbers and percentages taken from the Social Security Administration to give us a little more information about how the economic pie is sliced in America. To be in the

23. What Part Do You Play in Economic Justice?

top 1 percent of wage earners, you need to make over $250,000 a year, or $5,000 a week. To be in the top 50 percent of wage earners, you need to make over $30,000, or $625 a week. And here's a figure I'm not sure all voters are fully aware of: 48 percent of all Americans earn less than $30,000 a year. That means that almost half the population of the U.S. is living on less than $625 a week. What these figures tell us is that a little less than half of all American earners may be eligible for some form of government support.

Now let's look at how jobs and the people who perform them are valued.

In pretax income, the average truck driver in the U.S. makes about $765 a week, or $39,839 year.

The average teacher earns $1,084 a week, or $56,368 a year.

The average police officer earns $1,129 a week, or $58,708 a year.

During the same week that our average cop earns eleven hundred dollars, for every dollar the cop earns, the average hedge fund manager at a mid-level fund earns seven; in a single week, that's $6,730, or $350,000 a year. At the larger hedge funds, the average climbs to $46,000 a week or $2.4 million a year, according to the *2015 Glocap Hedge Fund Compensation Report*. Yet the hedge fund manager will pay income tax at half the percentage our cop pays.

The reason is that money made from investments is taxed at a far lower rate than money earned by salary. Salaried workers who exert their energy to create goods and services like the cop, the teacher, and the truck driver, their tax basis begins with 30 percent of their earnings. The hedge fund manager may pay only 15 percent on any part of income that is considered "capital gains," which is the result of stock transactions, accrued

27 QUESTIONS TO MAKE YOU SWEAT

interest, dividends, and income from any other bets the manager has placed on stocks or commodities (which is to say, most of his income). And as long as his money keeps making money, he'll be taxed at half the rate of the person who works as his administrative assistant.

The average pro basketball player in the NBA earns $95,576 a week, or about $4.9 million for the fifty-two weeks of the year. Yet the season is only about seven months long—almost nine if they go to the finals—so his value from his job gets extended in five months of non-basketball time, time he can use to turn his fame into more income, such as endorsing products, inspirational speaking, showing up at an instructional camp, and appearances on *Dancing with the Stars*! LeBron James makes $85.3 million a year when you figure in his endorsements. He stands to clear more than a billion in just sneaker bucks by the end of his career—a billion dollars for promoting shoes.

Why do we value a basketball player so much more highly than a schoolteacher or a cop?

Yet, among the very wealthy, pro athletes are a good example of how marketplaces should work, because they have quantifiable and valuable skills they exchange for better salaries—what's known as "merit pay" or "pay for performance": a major league baseball player who manages to hit twenty more homeruns than 98 percent of other major league players will be earning several multiples of their pay because those homers reliably win games. What they're paid for, really, is popularity. The more attention they attract, the more money they can command. But don't forget the owners who pay these salaries—they're making enough to pay *all the team salaries* and still fly in private jets and own islands. They're the real winners in the athletic popularity economy, but they are usually invisible.

23. What Part Do You Play in Economic Justice?

Back in the "working" world: if you're a really good school teacher, you might get amazing job satisfaction seeing more of your students accepted into college than your school averages, but it won't improve your salary. Instead, here's a nice Teacher of the Year plaque—now grade those papers!

But at the other end of the spectrum, for cats even richer than LeBron, the highest paid hedge fund manager, according to *Forbes* magazine, in 2018 made a grand total of . . . wait for it . . . 30 million, 769 thousand dollars *a week*, or a whopping $1.6 billion a year ($1,600,000,000 per annum for one person's energy). Give him the benefit of the doubt and say he works really hard—sixty hours a week, fifty-two weeks a year—that's still around *seven hundred thousand bucks an hour*. Hmm . . . that's a jolly $11,000 per minute; $183 per second—if, and only if, that person actually works sixty hours a week for fifty-two weeks a year. That was Jim Simons' yearly compensation for Renaissance Technologies in 2018.

For doing *what* that is so much more important than a teacher?

A hedge fund doesn't create goods or services; it places bets. Any investment is made as a bet or a hedge against profits. Not products—profits. Instead of investing in stocks to support a company's products or services, a good manager is just placing bets on their performance. While *investors* have a financial commitment to a corporation's success—and therefore the success of the whole manufacturing economy—a hedge fund manager has no loyalty to a company. (When you buy stock in a company, you can go long, which means you're betting on the stock going up in value and hence the company doing well, or you can go short which means betting the stock will go down or lose value.) Many hedge fund managers find ways to "short" their investment holdings—which means betting against the value of a company. How does hoping a company will lose money generate value for anyone but the manager and his fund investors? Is it possible that he (the majority are male) would use other investments to attack the value of a company he's shorting? It happens. This is why the world economy teetered on the brink of catastrophe in 2008—hedge fund profits from shorting had sucked too much money out of the economy.

That's how value and marketplaces work at the highest ends of the earning spectrum. Of course, when you're at the highest level of the economic ladder, you spend some of that free-flowing capital to make rules about the marketplace. You hire expensive lobbyists to convince Congress to help shape laws that favor you and your wealthy clients. Why do you think a hedge fund manager's profits are taxed at half the rate of salaried workers?

In case you're wondering if you—or anyone who isn't super wealthy—can get in on this hedge fund racket, fuggedaboutit. Such funds are exclusive clubs: membership is reserved only for those who can pony up with at least a $500,000 initial hedge fund investment. And those are minor league funds. You want to get into the majors with the big earners? That'll require a ten million initial investment to prove you belong in the club.

But let's continue to consider how the pie is sliced for the rest of us. How does our energy exertion compute in terms of economic reward and/or social benefit?

The average university professor earns around $1,880 a week, or $97,760 a year.

A head football coach in the SEC gets $4.1 million a year, or $78,000 a week (on average). But there's more icing on his (male again) cake. Every SEC coach also has perks and paid appearances as speakers and media personalities. Nick Saban,

23. What Part Do You Play in Economic Justice?

head coach of Alabama, made about $7.5 million, or $150,000 a week, in 2018, but at the end of the season, he missed out on a $800,000 bonus when Clemson whipped his team in the National Championship. Durn it.

Meanwhile the governor of Alabama got paid $191,000 for the whole year. But you know, they can both expense their dry cleaning . . .

There's no free dry cleaning for the average fast-food worker earning around $361 a week, or $18,800 a year. Unlike football players, they have to buy their uniforms from their salaries. But then, you don't have to take polyester to the dry cleaners, and technically, college football players don't get paid, no matter what the coaches get.

The average manicurist earns about $506 a week or $24,330 a year. Often these women (almost all are female) are required to work fifty or sixty hours for that $506/a week (which works out to around $11.70/ an hour.) This is pre-tip so with tips they can make another $250-300 which can bring their total to around $38,400 a year.

Salaried farm workers average $12.75/ hour, or about $25,000 a year. Entry level positions start at $20,241 per year, but with experience, farm workers can earn up to $42,266 a year. Most salaried farmworkers are immigrant laborers or first-generation Americans. Although the farmer may have inherited his farm, he can only make profits based on how much the land produces and how the markets value those crops. However, in 2018 those earnings have been crippled by the "trade war" the president deemed necessary. But for those who own the land, unlike poorer workers, the government makes special plans to ensure their incomes: they may get various forms of "crop subsidies" and other welfare payments by which they can be paid *not to grow* crops. That's called "money for nothing" in popular song.

Speaking of "money for nothing," many famous people find that they can turn fame into cash. Dr. Phil earns $79 million a year for his television "therapy," but he doesn't work the whole year, so he nets almost 3 million a week when he is working. Because he's famous, he can pad that with his name on books he's paid other people to write, special "celebrity" appearances, and of course, coffee mugs ($25 for the rare Dr. Phil blue logo mug).

Fame! Coach K, Mike Krzyzewski, head basketball coach at Duke University, makes a paltry eight million a year—that's $71 mil less than Dr. Phil—but he gets another $70,000 a night for speeches in the off-season. Not bad for a side gig. But wait, Usher commands twice that for his side gigs, say at your kid's bar mitzvah, but the kids love dancing to Usher . . .

Not every musician is Usher, however. The average professional musician—that's an average of the big stars plus all the rest of the professional class working in orchestras, or cruise ships, or sessions, or on the road—they earn $756 a week, or $39,312 a year. By contrast, the four members of U2 have each earned $500 million for the past ten years just on concert fees alone.

What about actors? The average "working actor" in the Screen Actors Guild earns $1,002 a week, or $52,104 a year. But wait, only 15 percent of the actors' union membership make the $16,000 a year required to qualify for health insurance. The other 85 percent have day jobs while they dream about scoring a lead on a Netflix series. Lotsa luck, crazy dreamers! But that 85 percent is still out there, waiting on tables, driving Ubers, going to acting classes, and working in commercials. Meanwhile, in 2017 Mark Wahlberg was the highest paid actor, grossing $68 million; that's $1.3 million a week, but Marky Mark didn't have

23. What Part Do You Play in Economic Justice?

to punch a clock for forty hours, fifty-two weeks a year. Not quite Dr. Phil money, but a lotta loot.

Unlike Dr. Phil, the average medical doctor earns around $185,016 a year, or $3,558 a week. Of course, "average" includes a gerontologist working in a clinic in Appalachia to the Hollywood plastic surgeon charging $2,000 per Co2 laser treatment to smooth away acne scars.

So those are the numbers. What do you think?

All these numbers are factual; they're drawn from the business community's own publications and from government stats. The dollar figures are pure data, without bias or judgment (despite the occasional snarky aside). Anyone can see who has dollars and how they expend their effort and energy to "earn" them.

This shows how much we value entertainment and fame. Football coaches earning fifty times what state governors make is a telling stat. But then, what does it tell us if a TV shrink is making almost ten times what the coach makes, which is more than we pay a group of fourteen hundred school teachers the same year? While those who are entertaining and famous may command our attention, when compared to other workers, are they really being fairly compensated for their skill sets? What part does luck play?

The top earners—who create no goods or services, who place bets in a marketplace they actively try to rig—are making far, far more than those who actually labor to create the essentials of the economy, from education to manufacturing to maintenance to services.

While fame and power are often well rewarded, the current situation is historically out of balance. The rich control much more money and more of the economy than they have at almost any other time in history.

27 QUESTIONS TO MAKE YOU SWEAT

Here's how it happened.

The American economy has, on the whole, done well over the past seventy years, but the wealth that has resulted from a mostly uninterrupted post-WWII boom has not been distributed equally among all Americans. This is easy to see: if all Americans shared in the prosperity, then the amount of dollars that both employees and CEOs are compensated should have gone up at the same rate. But what really happened? In 1967, according to the Economic Policy Institute, American CEOs of major corporations earned twenty-three times more than the typical worker. In today's dollars, that's $1,300 a week for the average worker and $30,700 a week per CEO, so the CEOs were well compensated. Yet in 2017, according to a headline in Fortune magazine, "Top CEOs Make More in Two Days Than an Average Employee Does in One Year." So even *before figuring* in their perks—which can quadruple their annual income—CEO income has risen well over 400 times higher than the workers in their corporation.

Or consider another historical marker: the rate at which worker versus CEO compensation increased in that same time period compared to productive output. In 2017 the median American household income was $61,000 a year—adjusted for inflation, that's a little less than $700 more per year than the median in 1999. And yet, over that *same eighteen-year time period*, gains in productivity—worker contribution—have increased the value in corporations 21.6 percent. The workers responsible for that production got a 1.8 percent salary gain over eighteen years of increasing their personal output, while the corporations—instead of raising wages—took hundreds of times that and paid it mostly to executives but also to stockholders. The workers got effectively zero compensation for their radically increased productivity, while executives made out like, well, bandits.

23. What Part Do You Play in Economic Justice?

If you think this seems unfair, you're not alone. Most American believe that something has happened to the U.S. economy that has detrimentally impacted the mass of low-end workers. Something did happen, but it happened very gradually and was sold to us as "less government and less taxes" over about forty years.

In the 1970s, politicians were successful in popularizing two political concepts: smaller and limited federal government along with more personal responsibility. Smaller and more limited government had enormous appeal in the aftermath of the Vietnam War. The Vietnam War had been perpetrated by a number of military and government lies and supported by a ballooning and bloated military budget. Personal responsibility became a code word for a reaction to Lyndon Johnson's "Great Society" that attempted to use government intervention to help level the playing field for poor and ethnic minorities. These two issues were extremely successful among the majority of white voters of every socioeconomic class. They marked a change in American politics that has since become distorted to empower only the wealthiest in society.

These political ideas were advanced and funded by ultra-rich conservative families and their associates who saw that this emerging distrust in government was an opportunity to woo voters—by using the vison of "less government"—but that actually meant less corporate regulation and lower taxes for them. These wealthy interest groups began to exert their influence in a concerted effort on several levels: they established "think tanks" made up of paid "theorists" who constructed strategies and arguments to try and influence certain election and legislative outcomes; they began buying and controlling news media with the specific intent to influence and change public opinion; they found new ways to use political action committees (PACs) to make end runs around existing campaign finance laws so as to be able to make game-changing political contributions, which they then leveraged into new laws that allowed them to make even larger contributions. At the same time, they invested dramatically more in lobbyists—often ex-legislators—to incite anger against social justice and other government programs.

This is a bit simplified, but all of it is easily vetted if necessary. Feel free to do your own research.

Thus, the idea that "something happened" consisted of all these objectively observable things, and they changed the national ethos of economic justice. Since the 1980s, this "neoconservative plan" has worked: the rich pay *radically reduced taxes* than in the 50s, 60s, and 70s. As a result the top 10 percent of earners now have super wealth, while wage earners increasingly struggle. At the extreme end, the top 1 percent of incomes now *own more wealth than the bottom 90 percent combined.*

One of the most successful campaigns the very rich have waged is to get control of the Supreme Court. This has been a huge win for them because the Supreme Court has subsequently decided that money is speech—a concept that would give any old-fashioned capitalist theorist whiplash and would certainly make all the founding fathers vomit in unison. This means that now the richest people can spend almost without limit for political influence, effectively "shouting" so loud that their "voices" are the only ones politicians hear. You may be aware that in the past twenty years it has become commonplace in certain circles for lobbyists to write a law and then hand it to their legislators, expecting it to be voted on the way they wrote it. Again, look it up.

Finally, the contributors with the deepest pockets get direct access to their congressional representatives, and as a result they often get special federal favors and tax breaks. Plus the American

23. What Part Do You Play in Economic Justice?

military protects their businesses and holdings in the Middle East, Latin America, and Asia under the guise of "protecting American interests."

Because this change has been gradual and sold as "less taxes for everyone"—which has not even been true—most taxpayers have no idea who pays how much or how their taxes are spent. They don't know that the rich don't pay payroll taxes, for instance, which is how social security is fully funded. They don't know how much the government borrows—a good chunk of it from China—and how much of their taxes go to pay interest on that borrowing. Nor do they have the faintest idea where there are cost overruns in government contracts—particularly in the military—that force both more taxation and more borrowing.

Instead, voters have been baited by political campaigns that someone else might be getting "something for nothing," such as foreign aid or food stamps, and that fear magnifies into a resentment of all taxation. They don't see what their taxes do *for* them—highways and bridges, schools that educate the workforce, clean air and water, police and EMS, hospitals, defense, communications infrastructure, safe workplaces, and so on. Worse, they think that foreign aid and food stamps suck up much of the budget. In fact, foreign aid and food stamps are a tiny percentage of what we spend on the military—which is, by the way, more than the military budgets of the next eight highest spending nations *combined*. There is no conspiracy to steal from taxpayers so the poor or other nations can profit.

The way taxes work, who gets taxed, and where the money goes should represent the conscious ethical feelings of the majority of the voters. That would be democracy. Yet it looks like the American government represents the minority with the money, not the majority of taxpayers.

27 QUESTIONS TO MAKE YOU SWEAT

Polls show that the majority of Americans approve of a government that looks out for everybody. Thanks to Medicare, old people don't have to die on the street. Thanks to food stamps, the poorest Americans can feed their family. However, because the will of the people has been subverted by fear-mongering and big-money propaganda, our government no longer performs the ethical will of the people.

The answer is not less government.

The government is only a network that organizes mutual support that should benefit all citizens. No one person exists outside the network of governmental support. No man is an economic island.

If we are going to see economic and social justice in America so that the national wealth falls more equitably to all income groups, we need to tax the wealthy realistically. It's pretty simple. In the 1950s and 60s in the United States, when middle-class families could afford a comfortable way of life on a single income, it was because Americans were sharing more equally in the economy, as evidenced by the income gap between rich and poor, which was at one of the lowest points in history. Why? Because the tax rate on people making over $300,000 was 91 percent. They didn't pay 91 percent on all their earnings—just earnings over $300,000. Below that, at every level of income, the tax rates were graduated so that everyone paid the same at every step up the earnings ladder. That was in 1959, and that rate didn't change for five years until it dropped to 77 percent in 1964 for any income over $200,000.

Let's take one of the wealthiest Americans in 1964, someone making a million dollars a year, easily in the top .01 percent of all income earners at that time. At the most they would have paid the federal government $670,000 in taxes. Fair taxation

23. What Part Do You Play in Economic Justice?

made every American's income grow proportionally to every other American's income. That's what makes it fair. Today that equivalent income is taxed at roughly half that rate, which is why the super-rich are getting super-richer. But before we compare the tax rates in 1964 and 2019, let's look at how the value of a dollar has changed so we can compare apples to apples.

In 1964, one dollar bought the equivalent of what $8.13 buys today. The value of the dollar has inflated by a factor of 8.13, so that same income of $1,000,000 in 1964 would now be an income of $8,130,000 dollars. Taxed at the 2019 highest possible income tax rate of 37 percent, our same millionaire today will pay approximately $3,008,100 in taxes.

This means that they get to keep approximately $5,121,900, whereas the 1964 person would be keeping, adjusted for today's inflation, $2,686,900. In other words, they're paying less than half the taxes as they would have in 1964.

The change in the tax laws have netted millionaires and billionaires massive tax savings, which have allowed them to accumulate wealth much faster than other income sectors. At the same time, this benefit for the wealthy has deprived the government of all those tax revenues and forced a higher tax burden on the middle class. It has also transferred tax burdens to more regressive taxes such as sales taxes, school taxes, highway tolls, and others that take proportionally more from poor people. This missing tax money has also caused a ballooning federal deficit (national debt) of a record *one trillion dollars* in 2019, which adds to an already 21 trillion dollar deficit and is projected to grow to *29 trillion* by 2028 unless our tax laws change.

This example of taxation is just one sliver of how our national ethos has been reengineered to favor the super-rich. To achieve social justice, it is the responsibility of every citizen to be alert to these changes and to fight for the true ethos of "equal treatment under the law."

The less "we the people" know and care about politics, the more "they"—the corporations and the one-percenters—can continue to pass laws that favor their agenda and cost the rest of us money. The more informed we are, the more we become motivated by educated self-interest and less by fear, the greater the chance we have to make changes that will elect and fund a government that supports and protects all of us. A government that supports "winner take all" means that the winners will indeed take all, leaving "we the people" with crumbs. That's not justice.

Sweat This Out

Consider the government goods and services you may be taking for granted: air traffic control, water purity, national weather service, highways, and bridges. Now, what if you get to keep all your money and you're in a world with no taxes and *none of these sorts of things that taxes buy?* Instead, you have to pay a corporation for every usage? *Hmm*...

How much toll would you pay every time you pulled your car on to the street?

Would you call the fire department if you knew it would cost you $1,400 per truck?

Education? Imagine paying a daily admission fee to get into the school building.

23. What Part Do You Play in Economic Justice?

Would you be willing to pay $500 admission to a national park?

What if the air were so polluted you couldn't go outside without an expensive personal respirator?

What if there was a flat fee of a thousand dollars to call 911 to report someone breaking into your house?

Take a look at your list of government services and consider that if you've decided to pay a corporation as you go, a significant percentage—usually 10 to 15 percent—will go solely to executive and CEO salaries. On the other hand, government workers and civil servants don't get salaries designated by their pals on the board of directors; they get the civil service pay scale. That's why, for instance, Medicare is so much more efficient than private health insurance: 10 percent to 15 percent executive savings off the top.

In your imagination, what does an "economically just" world look like? Should people pay for healthcare if it means they'll go bankrupt and have to sell their house? What if everyone received a minimum basic income to live on? What part does sharing, compassion, and generosity play in how you circulate money, how you imagine taxation, and how you spend your cash?

24. ARE YOU A FORGIVING PERSON?

Would you like to be more forgiving? The great South-African theologian Desmond Tutu has a great quote about forgiveness: "If you can find it in yourself to forgive, then you are no longer chained to the perpetrator." Not forgiving someone—holding grudges, harboring resentments, and seeking revenge—is like drinking poison and expecting someone else to die.

The ability to forgive is fundamental for a loving life. It's a skill we can develop, and if we are to listen to people like Desmond Tutu and pay attention to their sage advice we will enhance our life experience of both happiness and satisfaction by adapting a more forgiving attitude towards the difficult people in our lives.

I'm finishing a sandwich at my brother's cafe in downtown LA.
"So, Scott, I mean, you're forty-seven years old; you can't keep blaming Dad because you're unhappy. Try to forgive him. Let it go."
"No way. He was such an asshole and a horrible father. Why should I forgive him? He knows he fucked up."
"But all that was thirty years ago."
"But he was our father, our role model, and one day, he just leaves, no goodbye, no note, no nothing? And after that, he never does a goddamn thing to help me or you or Lizzie or Mom. He treated us like we were worthless."

"Don't you see that he was miserable? He was frightened of how bad he was failing us. He was fucking up his job. He knew he was weak. In his mind, he had no other choice."

"He's always known what he's doing; why should I forgive him? He's a master manipulator and a total narcissist."

"A narcissist is a sick person. Yes, he did horrible things, but I don't think he was capable of doing any better. Don't you see that your anger and blame thirty years later continues to give him power over you? He's infected you with his sickness—blaming. I'm just saying that if you could forgive a sick man for his disease, it might help you."

"What helps me is not talking to him and not seeing him. If he's dead in the Philippines, good. That helps me."

"That's pretty harsh, bro. All I know is that as long as I stayed angry with Dad, anything that went wrong in my life was his fault, so in some way, he was to blame. As I slowly forgave him for hurting me, I felt like I was growing up. I felt so much freer when I saw clearly that he was suffering as much as I was, and if I forgave him, all my suffering would go, too."

"You're so full of shit. You still get angry when you talk about him."

"No, I don't. You get angry when we talk about him, and then you go right to blaming him. But, Scotty, it's more than that. You're such an angry dude."

"I should be angry."

"If you're not angry with Dad, you're angry with someone else who's fucked you up. It's the same anger, and you hold on to it. You complain all the time. Your unhappiness is always someone else's fault, and Dad is the one you blame the most."

"You're so self-righteous. It really pisses me off."

"So now you're angry with me?"

24. Are You a Forgiving Person?

The ability to forgive people who have hurt us, emotionally traumatized us, disappointed us, or even physically abused us is essential to activate our power to love. I owe that insight to a book I read. I found *A Course In Miracles* on a shelf in a place called Awakenings, my favorite bookstore, and there was a lot of buzz about this book at the time. I heard it was a great book to finding a more peaceful soul, and because my sister and her first husband were in troubled waters, I bought it for them as a gift. They could use a miracle. I didn't bother to look inside because, hey, I'd already read a lot of life-changing books and thought I had a clue.

But a year later, I was visiting them and pulled it off the shelf. Surprise, surprise, it hadn't been opened, still brand new. Did my sister even read page one? I peeked inside, started reading, couldn't stop, and finally realized, *Damn, I bought this for myself.* Mr. Enlightenment gets a smack upside the head. What grabbed me was the completely fresh understanding of personal power it offered. It was actually a textbook, with a workbook at the end. The "course" was instruction in how to have the power to forgive everyone for everything all the time and how to live in a peaceful state of constant loving. Are you ready for that? I thought it sounded impossible too at first.

Until I read ACIM, I didn't even have the concept of that much forgiveness. "Forgiving everyone for everything all the time"? I mean, who does that? I'd have to forgive Hitler and Charles Manson and my father! Sure, I had some empathy skills; I could forgive some people for some things, but I also carried around a lot of blame and anger. I knew who had fucked me over and shouldn't they be . . . punished?

But as I read the book and did the exercises, I realized I was toting around an emotional suitcase full of conflicted feelings. In it were affection, friendship, curiosity, and other loving emotions, but filling up the rest of the suitcase were the razor blades and broken glass of rage, resentment, and blame. ACIM was a plan for unpacking, rearranging, and then getting rid of razors and broken glass to make room for more of the better feelings.

The Course helped me recognize that fear was the real root of my resentments, blame, and shame, and I learned that I could uproot fear, like weeding a garden. The weeds were just mistakes I and others had made, mistakes now safely in the past, and the only thing that kept them alive was reliving the old sense of fear and powerlessness. As long as I nurtured the old fears with guilt or bitterness, they'd choke my growth. Consciously forgiving people—because none of us are perfect—is like weeding the garden and making the space for more loving emotions to bloom.

It's a nice metaphor, but freeing a weed-choked garden (or unpacking a suitcase full of razor blades) requires real work and a keen attention to detail. Yet there's a problem: if all you know are weeds or razors, then you accept them as "normal"; it's the only story you know, so it's the story you tell yourself about yourself. In this story, you're always the victim of terrible forces or circumstances or people you have no control over.

Forgiveness means seeing that this "normal" story isn't really the truth. It means seeing from a different perspective and consciously rethinking all the emotions and motivations you remember.

I used to think that I was a very forgiving person, but really, although I was empathic and tolerant, I didn't get to the deepest levels of forgiveness—the levels that would free me from my painful baggage and allow me to grow past the habits of fear from childhood. That level of forgiveness wasn't something I knew how to do, but as I sat and allowed myself to be honest about the old fears, the anger, and resentment I still carried in my heart, I became convinced that forgiveness on that deep level was a skill

24. Are You a Forgiving Person?

that could be learned with practice and a method—just like any skill such as typing, cooking, or building furniture.

That book became my method: it tuned me in to how my anger and blaming my dad was a huge part of the story I told myself about who I was. I had been telling the story of what a terrible father I had and how as a kid I felt powerless and victimized, and as a result, I blamed him for what was wrong with me. It made sense: when he deserted us, he left our family broke and our feelings of family trust and love in a shambles. If I didn't have any money, it was his fault. If I had trouble with relationships, it was his fault.

Not only that, my story moved other people; they readily sympathized with "poor me," so I had a payoff of a certain kind of affection. But is pity really affection? The old fears that victimhood created in me made it seem reasonable that pity was all the love I deserved.

I felt stuck with the beliefs about myself that came from these bad feelings connected with my father. ACIM changed those beliefs by showing me that if I could look past the emotional memories and see the reality of what was actually going on, I could exchange my old feelings of fear and anger for new feelings of forgiveness and wisdom. If I could recognize that it was mental illness, not maliciousness, that was driving my dad, I could start the process of understanding and forgiving him. And then, and only then, I could stop repeating the past.

Once I started to connect with the possibility of forgiving my dad, other parts of my life also changed. I felt a need for more personal time; meditation and prayer became daily rituals. I also made time to do the exercises in the ACIM workbook. To be honest, reading that book has inspired me to write this book. I recommend that you check it out.

27 QUESTIONS TO MAKE YOU SWEAT

I'm not going to summarize the entire book here, but I do want to share a bit about how I became a more forgiving person. The more I sat in silence and the more I read ACIM, the more I internalized the constant reminder to "look for the love, look past the fear, forgive . . . look for the love, look past the fear, forgive . . ." This insight, over and over, built a new empathy in me, so I was able to imagine the pain that my dad must have been in—the reason he drank so much, the reason he lied, the reason he had to flee from those who loved and trusted him: he must have been in agony. Thinking this way caused my heart to soften toward him. I could see him as pitiful, not me, and that was the feeling of forgiveness.

It wasn't a process of "forgive and forget" but instead "remember exactly . . . and forgive." To transform how I was holding on to the past, ACIM gave me a new model of reality. I had been accepting that the emotional knot of my memories was the past: it was what it was and that's why I was who I was. But if I got back to the root memory and added in what I understood as an adult along with my intention to forgive, and then rethought those painful events, I could see clearly that there was a larger truth. My memories weren't necessarily reality; they were just a childish residue of what had happened.

As an adult with an intention to forgive, I could see there was much more to what had gone on. Instead of the residual emotions dictating the whole story, I could now tell a new story. I now knew more than my old fears and anger: I now could see that my father had made terrible mistakes—so I could retell a better story of my own life: a story of compassion, not victimhood.

Today, I can see that my father wasn't trying to hurt me; he was doing desperate things to save himself. When he was cruel or demanding with me, he was trying to teach me to be better than he was. I can forgive a desperate man for his cruelties.

24. Are You a Forgiving Person?

I won't claim that this has been an easy process. It was difficult, and at times, it brought up painful thoughts and memories, but *I was the one doing it*; it wasn't *being done* to me. I was getting control of my story even if I had to revisit the pain. I was rebuilding myself through the effort of forgiving.

Forgiveness is learning to take control of the storyteller's point of view, a point of view that transforms powerlessness to love, transforms old, automatic habits of fear and pain into lessons about how to grow through the pain, and then out of the pain. As the storyteller in the present, I have the power to see truths that I couldn't understand in the past. When we reexamine the story we tell ourselves about ourselves, we make the choice to see the truth.

How we interpret memory is a choice. Forgiveness is choice. Both are acts of storytelling. You can make the loving, creative choice, to heal yourself and heal the past.

When we begin the journey of forgiveness, we start to feel lighter, more expansive. Our present objectives become more attainable because we are no longer dragged down by the baggage we have been carrying for so long.

Sweat This Out

Think of the person in your life who has hurt you the most. Think of all the damage he or she has inflicted on you. Get out your notebook and make a list of everything this person did that hurt, disappointed, frustrated, or misled you. See if you can list fifteen insults.

Now think a little more deeply. Can you jot

down the times and places when you realized or felt the hurt? The more specific you can be, the better.

In the course of making this list, you may experience old emotions, or even newer, stronger, angrier emotions. Good! What's important is that you write down the details. It may take several passes, and some details or feelings may seem unimportant, but give this list a chance. Take some time, every day if you can, maybe even a week or two or three, to get to a complete list.

Once you have the list, pick the least bad thing. Can you see why your victimizer did it? What was motivating him or her? Set aside your hurt and try to see their need or fear. Thieves often rationalize stealing because they "need" the money more than you. They have the belief that someone stole from them.

The point of your list is not to forgive—no pressure for a result—but to take your experience out of the shadows and see completely what was going on, and then add just a little empathy. You are reconnecting to yourself at that time. You are seeing your victimizer precisely as they were, not as your memory of irrational cruelty.

That's all. Make the list; include the times and places. It's the first step.

24. Are You a Forgiving Person?

Forgiveness is an act of understanding first, empathy second.

And then slowly you earn the ultimate skill of compassion.

It's not easy; you can't force it.

You need to start.

25. HAVE YOU EVER INAPPROPRIATELY FORCED YOUR WILL ON SOMEONE? HAVE YOU YOURSELF EVER BEEN COERCED BY SOME KIND OF THREAT?

We shouldn't impose our wills on unwilling or weaker people, which is what the Buddha and Jesus taught. This could be an act of bullying, humiliation, or physical intimidation. Love is freedom and the granting of freedom. "Might makes right" is in the Fear Zone.

Two stories:

> Rolf had been my tennis coach since I was fifteen, so we had a good bond, a rapport. When one of his main pros—a guy named Michael—shredded his hamstring, Rolf called and asked me to come teach for him. He promised me beaucoup hours and what looked like the Big Money because the injury was going to take months to heal, and Rolf had a lot of wealthy clients he couldn't disappoint. But I had pretty steady work at another tennis club, so I told him no. I'd have to quit my other job on one week's notice right before the new season started, and I'd been at that club for a while, so I felt wrong about quitting on such short notice.
>
> My old coach Rolf said he was desperate, though, and he

offered me enough money to make my twenty-five-year old head spin. It was much more money than I had ever made, as well as more hours, and it was all happening so fast. I suggested to Rolf that we put our agreement in writing. His response was, "Gregg, it's me! You know me. We don't need a piece of paper." And so we didn't.

Things were great for about two months. And then...

"Rolf, this is completely unacceptable. Michael keeps taking his lessons back. Those are lessons you promised me."

"There's nothing I can do, Gregg. He's one of my senior pros, and the hamstring healed faster than anyone thought it would."

"There's definitely something you can do; you can tell him you promised me those hours until December. You're the director. You had an agreement with me."

"I'm sorry, Gregg. There's nothing I can do."

"Bullshit, Rolf. You promised me the work. I quit another job for you."

He turned his back on me and walked onto the court to teach his lesson.

Three hours later, I was getting out of the shower wondering what I was going to do for money. As I opened my locker, wrapped only in a towel, a hand grabbed me by the neck and pinned me up against the lockers. Rolf's face was inches from mine as he choked me. "If you dare say another fuckin' word about this, I will put your head through this locker. Do you fucking understand me?"

Story two:

Jessica and I had lived together in New York, but she moved back to Toronto saying she'd feel more secure and have more

25. Have You Ever Inappropriately Forced Your Will on Someone?

work in her hometown. We lived apart for a while, but then agreed that I should move to Toronto and live with her. I expected that things would go pretty much the way they had in New York, which from my perspective felt really good, but then she started complaining about me as though I were an invader. Things came to a head after dinner one night when she told me she felt like I was "always in the way."

I was confused. "When we were together at Christmas, I said very clearly that you should do what works best for you."

"I did, but now it looks like this'll just be like New York when all I did was cook for you every day and be there for you, and I was miserable half the time."

"But you wouldn't even let me do the grocery shopping. C'mon, why are you blaming me? I didn't pressure you. You decided we should live together up here, so I moved to Toronto."

"Bullshit, Gregg. Every time I called New York, you'd ask me when I was coming back. 'When are you coming back, baby? We should be living together. I really need you, baby.'"

"I don't think so. We'd talk and then, at the end of the conversation, we'd start missing each other, and you'd ask me if I wanted us to live together! I'd say, 'Of course I want to live together. I love you. But, Jess, it's got to be your choice.' It was your choice to move back to Toronto."

"I knew I shouldn't have listened to you. My parents told me; my sister warned me about you. I knew this was wrong."

"You said I should move in, so I came up here. It was on your terms. Now you're blaming me for being here. It sounds like you should be blaming your parents and sister. Or blame yourself for not listening to them."

"You are such an asshole." Her fist shot out at my chin, but I ducked, and it hit me in the back of my head, which really hurt.

And then she began pummeling my shoulder and my chest. I did my best to block her punches away from my face and got the hell out of the apartment.

In both these cases, I was on the other side of someone else's freak out. In both cases, I put myself in a relationship that my intuition had warned me against, but I was trusting people I thought loved me. I don't want to play the victim, but I do want to draw attention to how coercion happens. I wasn't a victim because I was locked in my own pattern of behavior that I didn't see at the time. We repeat patterns in our lives even when we feel they're wrong because they're familiar, even comfortable. The victim role can be a learned behavior, as can the bully role.

But becoming aware that something damaging is happening over and over again in a similar way that may constitute a pattern is a step toward stopping the repetition. And it works for both the bullied and the bully. It takes the intention to be honest to see the coercion.

In the case of Rolf, clearly he used the trust that a young student had for an admired teacher to coerce me into helping his business survive a crisis. He gave his word on our agreement, but when it suited his purposes, he used his power to renege. Worse, when I called him on it, he didn't have the integrity to admit that he was partially responsible for my decision to quit my other job and losing that connection, as well as not making the money he'd promised me. When confronted with his dishonesty, he physically assaulted me to force me to stop complaining, even though he knew my complaints were legit. Rather than meet me with the respect and honesty I deserved, he did what any bully does: he beat me up. He couldn't stand to be confronted with the dishonest image of who he really was.

25. Have You Ever Inappropriately Forced Your Will on Someone?

I finished the lessons on the schedule, and then I left his club and didn't speak to him for a number of years. But then he did what abusers often do and tried to lure me back into my old patterns with another job offer. When I reminded him that he choked me and threatened to bash my brains out, he shrugged it off and said, "Sorry, my bad." He claimed that he just lost his shit because I made him look bad in the club he ran. He said he was really sorry, and he told me he did honestly care about me and wanted to remain my friend.

I took the work because I liked the students and the pay, but I'll never trust him again.

With Jessica, I wasn't that smart. After she lit into me, I still stayed. I felt like I needed her. And while she never pounded on me again, it's not like I forgot. I always felt like she might attack me again. I thought I really loved her, so unlike with Rolf, I stayed. I told myself that she was worth it, so I could take it.

I was afraid I'd be lonely and incomplete without her. In fact, though, it was fear that was keeping me, not love. While there was some worry that she might tee off on me again, the thing that kept me there was the fear of being without her. I thought I needed her for my music, to feel like I had a home, and to be my friend and lover.

I never said anything about her smackdown. It was as if I were giving her tacit permission to beat on me "if she needed to." Clearly, she had a lot of frustrations she needed to vent, but it wasn't just with me; it also was with her parents and her sister. She felt like everyone was pushing her around, but she wasn't capable of honestly telling anyone how she felt. Because she was afraid of being honest with her family, she'd agree to do what they said and then resent it. Because I was the one she felt safest with, she acted out on me. I felt like I could take it, and by taking it,

27 QUESTIONS TO MAKE YOU SWEAT

I thought I'd be taking care of her and protecting her from her family's anger and humiliations.

But the truth was that I was opting into a cycle of abuse. Because I chose to stay, I wasn't a victim so much as a partner, and by staying, I was enabling my abuser. I had to be dishonest with my self-respect and with my own best interests to stay in the relationship. I was willing to trade my self-respect for my need for "love."

When we don't protect ourselves, when we don't voice our opposition to intimidation or bullying, we are tacitly accepting it—which is what I did with Jessica.

If we're not honest enough to say or do something about abuse, we end up acting out of acceptance and denial. Maybe we tell ourselves that we're strong enough to endure the manipulation and coercion in order to stay in the relationship, but who can accept being beaten? Yet after a beating, victims frequently rationalize the experience any way they can so they can stay in the relationship.

Bullies often feel shame and guilt, but they rationalize too. They see their abuse as impulsive: "It's not who I really am." There's always an excuse, often alcohol or lack of money, or just the question of who should be in charge, but it happens over and over again.

As long as both the abused and the abuser accept the hurtful behavior as somehow "necessary for the relationship," the abuse will never stop.

Yet both parties know it's wrong. And both bear some responsibility.

25. Have You Ever Inappropriately Forced Your Will on Someone?

Sweat This Out

Part one: do you remember a time when you used coercion or humiliation to get your way? Or physically forced someone to do something? A shout or a shove? Perhaps a threat? Think about your childhood or college, or anything related to intoxication, even if you don't have a complete memory. Go ahead, make a list.

Part two: have you ever been abused, forced to do something against your will? To cheat in a game, to go sexually further than you wanted to? To lie, manipulate, cover for someone else? Make the list. When and why did these things happen?

Part three: do any of your current relationships rely on intimidation or the use of fear in transacting wants and needs? Think about work as well as personal relationships.

Part four: do you know any people around you who use coercion: friends, lovers, family, bosses, employees, neighbors who you have seen traffic in dishonesty, violence, or fear? Put them on the list too.

Look hard; try to find the courage to be completely and fully honest. Once you begin thinking about it, it may take weeks before you can fully answer these four questions.

26. WHAT IS UNCONDITIONAL LOVE?

Have you ever loved anyone unconditionally? Unconditional love is a difficult relationship to get our heads (and hearts) around. Love without conditions, pure acceptance, without the bargaining of "you must give me something and then I will love you" is very rare. At its most extreme, it's what saints do: they can love their tormentors.

Unconditional love is mature love, it's generated by the self, and it's both accepting and responsible. Unconditional love is actually true freedom, and true freedom is the direction we all want to grow in. That might sound a bit mystical, it is, but let me try to make it clear.

> I had just gotten home from a long rehearsal. Lena was on the phone with Dan again. She was just hanging up when I got out of the shower.
> "Lena, it really bugs me that you keep talking to Dan."
> "I've told you a thousand times, he's just my friend. You know he's my yoga teacher."
> "It seems like you talk to him more than you talk to me."
> "You're so jealous. What happened to your unconditional love?"
> "'Unconditional love' means I watch my wife have an affair in front of my face?"

27 QUESTIONS TO MAKE YOU SWEAT

"You're so dramatic. No one is having an affair."

"You text Dan ten times a day, you have private yoga sessions with him that last for hours. I feel neglected."

"Oh my God, when are you going to give up on this thing?"

"You want me to let it go, but you're not just talking once in a while. You've got a nonstop text-festival, even when I'm in the room."

"Enough. You and I aren't fused at the hip. I have a life; I want to talk to other people once in a while. I need other people in my life to balance me out. Just let it go. You're the one putting conditions on our love."

"Don't you unconditionally love me?"

"When you act like this, I don't."

For the most part we live in a world of conditional loves; it's love by contract. We agree to love one another as long as *certain conditions are met*. It doesn't matter if the love is romantic, familial, platonic, or patriotic; there are certain roles that are required to create the feelings of love. We have agreements that define the person we love as special, and in so doing, we get to be special. We have definite expectations about what we will get and what we will give, and those expectations of giving and getting are the conditions that create a safe space and enable us to open up and feel the security of love.

There's just one little problem: such security-creating conditions are fear-based. If there's fear, it's not love. Unconditional love is love without fear. It comes from complete security without making a deal. And it's really difficult to do!

To love without expecting something? To love without fear? Is it even really possible to love unconditionally?

Let's put a lens on what "unconditional love" might mean to

26. What Is Unconditional Love?

us as adults by reviewing some recent psychological studies in the neuroscience of happiness. These studies have found that babies raised with constant attachment to a parent (usually the mother) for the first two years of life, including carrying the infant during daily life and sleeping with the child at night, are often more stable, more grounded, and more capable of maintaining long-term relationships into adulthood than children raised by more physically distant parents. As a result of the security-creating love, they're more able to love with absolute trust and freedom in their adult relationships. Because they felt this unconditional love as infants, they are more likely to create it as adults. And considering what a baby requires 24/7, unconditional love really means, metaphorically speaking, "accepting another person with all their shit, pee, and puke."

This is not meant as an indictment of parents who don't do this or of anyone who loves conditionally; it's just a basis for beginning to think about the value of loving this way. People who can love unconditionally are generally happier. And happiness is the key to a good life.

If we accept that the ability to love unconditionally is worth developing, then those of us who didn't get unconditional love in infancy need to develop this power within ourselves after those formative years have passed.

When I was a younger man, I thought I understood unconditional love; Lena and I even agreed to put it in our wedding vows. And I think I was typical. Most of us think our ability to love is "pure," or "natural," or "total," or "true," and we mistake these love-song clichés for "unconditional." I certainly did. But I was wrong.

I hadn't really figured out how afraid I was—afraid that I'd lose love or be hurt by love, afraid on a fundamental level that

I was unlovable. That was why I wanted to put "unconditional" into the marriage vows; it was a guarantee for this magnificent love I thought we were capable of. Yet a guarantee is a condition. Vowing to love in a certain, defined way and then later calling on that definition to enforce behavior—damn, that's not unconditional at all.

This is why it's such a tricky business. Can you still love if the person you love is doing terrible things? Can you love even when you're not loved in return? Can you still love when you feel lonely and isolated?

The fact is: love is a skill.

Wait! Love is a skill? WTF?

Don't we just love "naturally"?

The short answer to that one is "no way."

"Nature" is what we're evolutionarily disposed to do: a.k.a. human nature. Using the previous model of unconditional parent/infant love, let's look at how evolution has designed us to learn to love.

Human babies evolved like all other primates, being constantly carried by or close to their mothers, and so every infant is designed to feel that constant contact we talked about earlier. Take it away, and on some level, the baby senses that something is wrong—a feeling of unnatural vulnerability, loss, abandonment. Unlike other primates—and unlike the first thousands of years of the species *homo sapien*—we don't live as foraging tribes; modern *homo sapiens* live in nuclear-family houses. What does this mean to infants? If modern parents reject the choice of putting their stinky, messy baby in their bed and instead they put the kid in a crib or in another room, they don't think they're "abandoning" their baby. "It's the way we do things" in our current culture, even if it's not the way we used to behave. Yes, it may be planting the

26. What Is Unconditional Love?

seed for some insecurities, but it's still a whole lot more loving than, say, the Victorians or the Spartans, two cultures who beat the hell out of kids to "toughen them up."

I don't think the scientific community has any conclusive studies on this idea yet, but I believe it has valid merit in terms of how we learn to love. Human infants evolved for hundreds of thousands of years being carried by Mom for almost two whole years, and in just the last couple thousand, we've been experimenting with dumping the infant in a cradle so that constant contact is gone, and that builds into us a latent message that persist into adulthood: love is conditional.

The baby is too young to understand much, but she will "feel" her evolutionary design for constant security and warmth. If she is kept secure and warm until she's able to walk and eat by herself, she will develop a certain confidence, the most basic sense of self-esteem. Because she's been constantly secure while learning locomotion, language, and relationship skills, at a certain point, when she *wants* to get loose from Mom, she will waddle off, secure in the knowledge that Mom (and usually the rest of the clan) will be around if she falls. Because she's been constantly and unconditionally loved, she feels confident that she's capable on her own and knows that she's loveable; she has a sense that "I'm OK." She also feels secure in giving that unconditional love back.

In contrast, consider the development of children who are put away from Constant Mom and out of the center of their parents' lives. That same evolutionary need for security and warmth is only met occasionally, so this baby will develop differently. While putting the baby in a crib or a separate room seems to work out well enough (for the parents), it disrupts the "natural" development of a secure feeling of being "loved." Instead of

27 QUESTIONS TO MAKE YOU SWEAT

Mom being there for pain or hunger, the baby has to cry, has to wonder where the warmth is, has to endure prolonged feelings of fear or hunger or hurting alone. Think of how that affects her young nervous system when fear and pain must be endured for longer periods of time than her nervous system is evolutionarily designed for. The intercom and baby monitor are not the same thing as Mom's constant presence. A crying baby is really in a state of panic; she has a sense of intense vulnerability, and so this child develops a different sense of who she is and how confident and loved she is. This example is to help us understand how the way we are able to love develops from early relationships and baby and parent signals. It's a bit simplistic, but it's a way of looking closely at a process that each of us has gone through and thinking about how our emotions and ideas of love develop. Using the model of constant primate mothering as a baseline, you can see how and why modern children develop differently; yet because the infant can't express herself or explain feelings or memories from this part of life, the development will still seem "natural." "Everybody does it"—or they don't: even today some children are raised with almost constant parental contact, and those children later in life will be more able to love unconditionally.

For the rest us who didn't get that level of attention, the infantile episodes of fear may turn into a baseline of adult insecurity. Instead of that "I'm OK" confidence that love will be a constant presence, as adults we may fret that love may not show up. Just like that crying baby felt, we may wonder, "What's wrong with me? Why am I alone and miserable?"

This sense that something is wrong with me is a feeling that I need to meet a condition to get love. I should do or be something more than I am to ensure that love will constantly be there. If we're raised with this kind of conditional love, it's all we know. It

26. What Is Unconditional Love?

then becomes what we expect. We think it's "natural," and this feeling permeates our unconscious to where we think that all love is conditional. The condition of earning love by performance ends up feeling natural.

This behavior of earning attention that feels like love—unless we consciously address it—is the basis for lifelong anxiety and insecurity. The parent-child relationship is the model by which we create ourselves in daily life. Yes, perhaps people raised with strict conditional love are attention-seeking successes: earning money, gaining professional accolades, possibly becoming religious or political leaders, but they are constantly striving to be loved by trying to meet the demands of those conditions.

But here's the good news: even if we didn't get constant unconditional love as an infant, our minds have the inclination to understand what that might feel like, and we can develop it. If we've experienced even bits of unconditional love from parents who love and forgive us, even if there wasn't a constant infant connection—we *can learn* to forgive ourselves. As adults, if we know what the model is, we can grow in the direction of unconditional love.

The problem of not understanding unconditional love is that as long as we're conforming our lives to meet other people's conditions and imagining that we'll only be loved by meeting those conditions, we live under the imaginary scrutiny of others' approval. We almost can't feel good about ourselves until someone else approves of us ("loves" us). That conditionality undermines our confidence, which prevents us from feeling we are in the moment, free and spontaneous. Waiting for validation, approval, or someone's "love" means that we miss out on the joy. Why "joy"? Joy is the emotion of unselfconscious pleasure. If you can feel joy, you have a purchase on unconditional love.

The preliminary step to fully understanding unconditional love is observing our joyful selves.

If we are to unconditionally love ourselves, we'll need to heal that fundamental insecurity—the destructive urge to earn love by performing for someone else's expectations. One possible strategy for healing is getting away from the family. You don't have to separate completely and forever, but long enough to get perspective, to see your family for the network of expectations and agendas that families tend to be, which we all call "love." But it's not necessarily healthy love; it's affection on the condition that you perform the role your family imposed on you—whether that's going to law school or winding up drunk in a gutter. It's all about family values!

Physical distance will help. Going to college is often an opportunity to see one's family more honestly. Having your own job; traveling to different cultures; an intense spiritual practice; dating people who make your parents uneasy—these are all symptoms of degrees of separation. To heal, you need to start by recognizing what conditions you've been willing to perform for and come to think of as natural in order to receive love. That won't automatically mean that you can instantly stop the performance, but you have to see the *why* of what you're doing first—the conditions you're putting on yourself—before you're able to know and love your authentic self.

Your authentic self is confident that you are lovable without anyone's conditions and rules, and it feels authentically loving toward the world as well. Because this love is self-generating and self-sustaining, it's totally independent. This is freedom.

Unconditional self-love—real freedom—could be criticized as selfishness: if you unconditionally love yourself, aren't you just making yourself feel good all the time and to hell with other

26. What Is Unconditional Love?

people's feelings? No. Unconditional self-love is self-acceptance, not narcissism. Narcissism justifies doing anything to anyone to service and pleasure the self. It is an "unconditional" state, but it is not love. It's not even self-love; instead it's a kind of pathological selfishness that doesn't feel or value connection to others. It's all about ME, muthafuckas!

That's not what I'm talking about. Unconditional love for oneself is the prerequisite to being able to love others unconditionally. That confident nurturing of the self and honoring the alliances we have with others is what empowers us to love without demanding anything in return. The nature of love, then, is not essentially pleasure-seeking but nurture-creating. Simple-minded pleasure-seeking is like eating the jelly donut and triple mocha Frappucchino for every meal; nurture-creating is enjoying a range of flavors in a healthy diet, possibly even enjoying the food shopping and preparation, and at its most powerful, sharing this whole process with friends and lovers and honoring all appetites. Love as nurture means controlling your impulses and making choices to create that sense of freedom and joy for everyone. When we dance together, joy creates joy.

The real freedom of unconditional love comes from security. Security begins from feeling a heart connection to all aspects of life. We feel we're in love with love, the creative, nurturing energy that exists in nature. That's the feeling the saints have when they forgive their tormentors. That same unconditional awareness means that we're also much more able to accept others unconditionally, and they get the vibe to feel free to be who they are, too, with all their strengths and weaknesses. What could be more nurturing? Or really, more joyful?

If we are to move from *conditional* love of self—where we judge ourselves based on others' values—to *unconditional* love of self—where we create our lives based on what nurtures and satisfies us—that transition requires healing the past and developing courage for the future. In other words, it requires work. It takes learning to have the courage to be honest in an often dishonest world, and that degree of honesty gives us the power to see and own who we really are—when the world—family, job, school—is constantly seducing and compelling us to compromise our authenticity.

Until that healing occurs, our unconscious selves will habitually be attracted to conditional judgments our family and cultural experience have guilted us into, and these will feel "natural." We need to recognize when we feel compromised, so we can do better.

One of the key opportunities in life that offers us the chance to work on unconditional love is the formation of a serious romantic pair-bond. Author and therapist Harville Hendrix believes that unconsciously—as a reflex—we fall in love with people who duplicate our primary caregivers' weaknesses as well as strengths. Hendrix's research and experience with many years of couples' therapy has shown that the true magnets that attract us to our partners and solidify the connection are our insecurities and failings. When we're first attracted to someone, our unconscious is looking to recreate the relationship dynamic we have had with our primary caregivers, so we look for the same *conditions* that we first learned were love. If they were dysfunctional and misguided, we're going to attract that kind of love "naturally"—unless we do the work.

If you've had relationships fail, the work of self-awareness leading to unconditional love is to see why those failures happened and to see *your part*. If all you do is blame your partner, the chances are good that you'll recreate dysfunction in your next relationship because you haven't grown from the experience.

26. What Is Unconditional Love?

If you're in a troubled relationship now, Hendrix would say it's an opportunity to do the work of healing. I would encourage you to ask one question before you decide to take that path of healing with your troubled relationship: "Am I in love with this person enough to be willing to open myself up and change behavior, even if it's possibly an uncomfortable change?" Both partners have to agree to be willing to change, however. If it's a yes for both of you, by all means get to work. If it's a no from one of you, it might be time to start packing. Moving toward unconditional love means acknowledging destructive conditions in the relationship. If one person believes he or she is right and thinks the other person needs to change, that's usually the most basic destructive condition. When a person isn't open to changing dysfunctional, misguided behavior, there is no chance for growth. Ideally you're both growing in the direction of unconditional love.

This process requires that radical honesty we were talking about earlier. Instead of hiding our authentic thoughts, desires, and fears, can we lovingly speak them? It can be difficult to speak the truth of our own experience, as well as painful to hear the truth of our partner's experience. But it's important that we take full responsibility for who we are and take the time to fully understand who our partner is. It will hurt because we are already invested in illusions and conditions, and like all habits, they will be difficult to give up. We have to try and see the way the destructive conditions we learned earlier have compelled us to hide our true selves.

When couples make the commitment to change and go to a place of absolute, radical honesty about how they feel—*this is the work*. This freedom of expression and mutual nurturing makes it possible to reignite the feelings of love and passion that were a part of the intense attraction that we experienced at the start of the relationship.

So much of our personal reality is taught, and the power of the habits we develop is immense; in fact, we may even believe that they work *for us*, if only because we've survived for as long as we have. But it's possible to survive in misery. It's possible to survive in cruelty. Both misery and cruelty are conditions of slavery. When you bow to your habits of conditional love, even when you are only distantly aware that they aren't nurturing, you're still their slave. But if you can honestly admit to your discomfort and honestly want to change, you will discover the strength and courage to break your chains.

26. What Is Unconditional Love?

Sweat This Out

A thought experiment: Take time for yourself away from other people; go to a place you feel safe and won't be interrupted, and then turn off your devices and think about a person in your life with whom you have a troubled love relationship. It could be any version of love—lover, mother, father, sibling, offspring, friend.

Envision that person sitting with you. See their face: relaxed, open, and ready to listen to whatever you have to say. Tell that person the truth about your feelings, the whole truth and nothing but the truth. Recount stories of what hurt you, how you felt let down or humiliated. Tell them about the times you were frustrated and angry. Recall when they acted out in extreme emotions.

You want to visit every troubling aspect you can think of. And imagine that they just listen.

Next, confess to everything you have done to hurt, torment, humiliate, manipulate, undermine, or otherwise disrespect this person. Imagine them listening, nodding, and hearing you out.

That's it.

Just try to be completely honest.

(This is not something you want to do with an actual person—at least not until you've had practice with this exercise and start to feel a sense of forgiveness . . . for both of you.)

27. WHO IS THE MOST POWERFUL PERSON ON THE PLANET?

Could it be the president of the United States? Jeff Bezos, the richest person in the world, owner of Amazon? The pope? The Dalai Lama? Or your mom? Your boss? Your spouse? The "most powerful person"—what does *power* even mean?

Perhaps you feel that you never have enough power, but other people do—the religious clergy, the rich, your boss or your relatives, celebrities, the government . . . perhaps you think all of them have more power than you, and/or power over you. How do they manifest their power? And what do you do to manifest your power?

When you consider who might be the most powerful person in the world, consider this: where does your—or anyone's—power come from?

> *I was sitting in Mr. Klein's office staring at him across his half-acre mahogany desk.*
>
> *"I will never forgive you, Gregg. I will never forgive you for taking my son away from me and destroying my family."*
>
> *"I didn't 'take' Josh anywhere. I argued with him to stay here and work out his stuff with you. I never wanted him to go out west and join that community."*
>
> *"You were the one that got him on this ridiculous spiritual*

path, whatever the hell that is. Trying to 'find himself'—what kind of horseshit is that? I know who he is. He's Josh Klein, and he belongs with his real family, the Klein's, not some new 'cosmic family' with a new name. He wants me to call him Ezekiel Hozannah? Who the fuck is Ezekiel Hozannah?"

"Ezekiel is still Josh, and Josh is still your son. And hey, that's between you two. I'm here now. I'm still here talking to you. I'm not living out there. Your blaming me misses the point. You created this too. You were pretty rough on him when we got back from the Caribbean, when he started sharing his feelings of spiritual growth."

"He started smoking pot, handing out tracts for Jews for Jesus. I mean, come on, Gregg, what did you do to this kid's mind?"

"What did I do? You've been his father for twenty-seven years. Josh and I have been really close for a couple of years, and we went on vacation for a week. How can I possibly have had more influence than you?"

"You're the one who put cockamamie ideas into his confused brain. He trusted you and listened to your garbage, and now 'Ezekiel' has moved across the country to be with a bunch of hippies that worship some space-alien Jesus."

"My beliefs are not 'garbage,' and they're not the same as Josh's. Josh's reasons for moving are his alone. I argued against it. It's not what I wanted, and it's really not what I believe."

"Of course, it's what you believe. You're always talking to me about Jesus and how much you love him."

"For me, Jesus was a very loving guy, and yeah, he's a model I like to use, but there's many Jesuses out there. You're his dad—did you really try to listen to him when he told you about his faith?"

"It was all horseshit, this crap about his spiritual body."

27. Who Is the Most Powerful Person on the Planet?

"But it sounds like you're blaming me because Josh has ideas you can't control."
"You have ruined my life, and I will never forgive you."

In this true story, Mr. Klein, a billionaire, a member of the wealthiest 0.1 percent and the kind of person many of us believe to be very powerful, seemed to argue that he had less power than his son's friend who was also the family tennis coach.

Mr. Klein imagined that power came from "out there," and when his son started saying and doing things he didn't understand, he felt vulnerable and afraid because he had no confidence in his own power.

Actually, there was a bit of truth in what he claimed. Josh and I had been good friends, and for a time we shared a path of spiritual discovery. Our discoveries changed both of our lives, and for Josh, that meant that he reconsidered his "family values" and the traditions he'd been raised with. Josh and I both influenced each other's spiritual insights, and we had shared some real joy. Neither of us directed the other; we shared.

And yet, when Mr. Klein saw his son's new behaviors—when Josh began to say things and do things that he disagreed with, he became so fearful that he belittled Josh's new beliefs and tried to intimidate his son. Mr. Klein demanded that Josh "stop all this spiritual nonsense" and conform to their family values. When Josh tried to explain his new feelings—joyful feelings—Klein accused him of being crazy and tried to take control of every aspect of his life. He insisted that Josh move back into the family home and check in with him daily.

Josh was hurt and angered that his father would so disrespect him and be so dismissive of the deep spiritual feelings that had awakened inside of him. He told me, "My dad is so blinded by fear that he doesn't recognize his own son." Partly because of his father's anger and accusations, Josh made the choice to move away and start life anew in a place where he felt he'd be recognized and loved.

After Josh left, I had come to talk to Mr. Klein to see if I could help get them back together. But instead, Mr. Klein began blaming me—after all, Josh and I had had long discussions about faith and love, so obviously I had "infected" his son with poisonous ideas.

Like Josh, I was dumbfounded by his aggressive accusations. I hadn't changed Josh. Josh changed Josh. I tried to tell Mr. Klein that I had actually advised Josh to stay and try to work things out, but Josh had had enough of being treated like a child. He felt like he had to get out of his father's sphere of influence, and that was a big part of why he moved across the country to live with a new community. In contrast to the way his dad was treating him, Josh's new "family" supported each other in their faith. Yes, it was their version of Christianity, but it was an environment that Josh felt was nourishing to his soul. Now, eighteen years later, he still lives there happily.

Mr. Klein didn't hear a word I said about how he might reconnect with his son by listening to him and giving him a little respect. He only wanted to blame me for Josh's decision.

Going back to our question of who is the person with the power, Josh took the power to determine his own life. Yes, he also made a radical choice, but only after his father's fear of losing his son made him attempt to control him; that was the very thing that drove him away. Josh made some very hard choices along the way. He chose to have spiritual power over material power, giving up a very substantial trust fund in favor of a loving community with far less financial security.

27. Who Is the Most Powerful Person on the Planet?

Mr. Klein only saw Josh as a defector from the family belief system. And then the worst thing happened: all his money couldn't force his son to give up what he truly believed. When his financial manipulations failed, Mr. Klein slipped into a panicky fear—money wasn't the real power after all.

When Mr. Klein and I had our talk, he felt he'd lost his son forever, but he couldn't credit Josh with having real power—that would be too devastating. Therefore, in keeping with his image of his son, he had to blame me. In his mind, two powerful beings had struggled for control of his son, and somehow he'd lost to me. In essence, he imagined that I, the family tennis pro, had power over Josh and thereby, power over him, a billionaire. His belief about power was that it was all external—it was money, me, religion, and Josh. All his worst fears of loss were being realized: he was losing his son, his money had no effect, and a lowly poor person with an idea about love and spiritual life had started it all. It was happening to him, but he couldn't see that his upset came from his beliefs about power, not from Josh or me.

It wouldn't be fair if I didn't acknowledge the fact that with all these ideas about power and how he viewed power, Mr. Klein was also just incredibly upset about losing his son to what he believed was some kind of cult. My perception was and is more along the lines of a community of like-minded individuals that choose to live and work together with a very strong-willed leader with definite opinions that sometimes border on the far-out. From what I learned about that community, everyone that lives there has chosen of their own free will to be there, and they can stay until whenever they choose to leave. That doesn't feel like a cult to me.

Mr. Klein's misery is what happens when we imagine that power is "out there." But what if it's all "internal"—within ourselves? What if it's not so much about what happens to us, but what we decide we'll do with what happens? What if real power comes from ideas and imagination? And that's part of the discovery that Josh and I were sharing; together we imagined creating a better world by living with a more loving mindset. We bonded around ideas of love and community, a world where wealth is shared more than hoarded. Josh acted on his ideas and felt a new satisfaction with his own power and choices.

Mr. Klein believed that Josh shouldn't be a free agent, using his mind to make critical choices; instead he thought his son should be an unquestioning minion, more like a possession. Which is not surprising, given that Klein's energy was devoted to accumulating material power.

If we were to ask Mr. Klein, "Who is more powerful, me or you?" and if he were to respond honestly, it's not him, the billionaire, but me, the tennis pro and his son's spiritual compatriot. And really, it's not even me the person; it's my ideas and imagination.

We're back to the question of what power truly is. How do you get it?

If you are alive, you have power. How much is up to you. It may not seem that way if you're in debt, if you're struggling to feed your family, if you're still living at home. But if it really comes from your ideas and imagination, we can build a simple model from there.

Our power in being alive has two dimensions: we have time (even if we never know how much), and we have energy (which may vary). In these two ways, we're all the same: our power is essentially the product of how we use time and energy.

We can take it a step further: we tend to spend our energy and time doing those things we believe will create more "power."

27. Who Is the Most Powerful Person on the Planet?

Some of us spend time and energy getting money, others spend time and energy in service, others on their family duties, and still others are artists spending time and energy creating new things. Although the form the power takes differs, each of us believes that we're gaining more power, and that power is a factor of time and effort. You might say, "But I have *no time* at all because I'm so busy earning money." Yet your day has the same twenty-four hours that mine does; it's just that you spend your time doing what you believe is essential for your power to survive. Yes, we all need some money to survive, but after surviving, how are we spending our life force?

The key to your power is how you direct your time and energy. How you spend your time is an indicator of where you believe real power resides. We create our idea of what power is in our mind; it's an internal event. We use our imaginations and ideas to design our lives—how we spend our time and energy—to *create* more personal power.

What is the purpose of personal power?

The most fundamental good that our power creates is simply that we survive (big shout out to Abe Maslow!). To secure our survival, we do what we need to do: forge relationships, get jobs, find shelter, look for safety in the world. Think of the "fight for survival"—everyone has a survival plan to fill their most basic needs. Some of us may live in refugee camps, while some might live in palatial homes with sweet jobs and a daily massage; but for all of us, survival is the beginning place for the ongoing negotiation between the world out there and the ideas in our minds, our true power source. Some of us will have more brutal and immediate negotiations than others, but in any case, if we don't survive, our power source dies. The first test of ideas and imagination is survival.

Then, after we have secured our survival, for what do we use our power? Here's the real test of individual power: what we create with our energies after survival will determine how much power we feel we have. Ultimately this is how we will answer the question: Who's the most powerful person in the world?

You've got survival handled. You're alive and reading this. Great. You're probably not in a refugee camp. However, even a refugee who is barely surviving is capable of tremendous personal power. A reporter from an American magazine was in a refugee camp in Sudan. It was grim. People were barely surviving, relying on aid, lining up for food and water, living in tents.

The reporter saw a skinny guy with a big smile on his face. The reporter introduced himself and asked the smiling refugee why he was so happy when he was hungry and thirsty and close to so much death and misery.

The guy said, "Walk with me."

As they walked, the guy kept picking up odd stuff. Sometimes he'd pause to look at a branch or a bag, apparently trash on the ground. When they got to his tent, it was full of art that he'd made from these objects. "I'm happy because I live in such beauty," he said. His ideas and imagination were more powerful than his circumstances. He didn't live in blame or fear. He lived looking for beauty, and in the process, he was a good comrade to those around him who were suffering. And he gave his art away.

Compare his power to Mr. Klein's. Our refugee-artist was constantly creating his life through a sense of wonder and beauty. It made him the sculptor of his existence. Although his survival was jeopardized by circumstances beyond his control, he refused to be victimized; he chose to control those things he could and celebrate the fact that he was surviving by finding beauty in a place where no one else could see it. His circumstances were

27. Who Is the Most Powerful Person on the Planet?

infinitely more terrible than Mr. Klein had experienced with his disobedient son, yet he knew he was creating his world through his own ideas and imagination, and he could smile and share. He could come from a place of love when the world around him was riven with fear. Clearly, he was the most powerful person in his world.

And this is the power we all have.

Am I the most powerful person in the world? If you ask me, I'd say yes, I am potentially the most powerful person on the planet.

But so are you.

Our sense of our internal power determines how we feel about ourselves in the world. It's not what's happening to us, but what we do with what's happening. Each of us has a degree of control over our feelings, depending on how mindfully we see ourselves and the world. If, no matter how bad I might feel—in pain, penniless, "in disgrace with fortune and men's eyes," as Shakespeare described it—if I can still find love in my heart for you, for the sunset, for birdsong, for the trash on the ground that I transform into art, or for being grateful for having been alive up to this moment—then that *feeling* is my power.

This is the exact inverse of the way the culture at large defines power for us—as always "out there," as money, influence, or celebrity status. But if power is "out there," then we have only two choices in life: spend our time getting it or protecting ourselves from it. If all power is external, it's logical to imagine that any power we don't access or don't understand means we must defend ourselves against it—perhaps even destroy it. In setting up that adversarial relationship, we imagine that there must be "evil" in the world. That evil is "their" power.

Who are "they"?

"They" is anyone we disagree with, who looks different, who is not in "our tribe," who comes from another country, or maybe even a different socioeconomic group. Anyone who roots for the Red Sox.

It's clear that the most powerful person in the world is the one who decides what evil is, the one who decides what's good and bad, the "theys" that enact laws to dictate what they have declared is right and wrong, bad and good, what we should fear collectively, whether everyone agrees or not. If you believe that power is out there, you are creating a constant anxiety, a fear factor for yourself; it's in your imagination and your ideas—you're creating it.

You can create another way of imagining things.

Here's Shakespeare again from Hamlet: "There is nothing either good or bad but thinking makes it so." The world itself is fairly neutral to each of us as individuals, in the sense that so much of what happens to us is about how we perceive it. We're all born into different circumstances that one could argue are not neutral, and I would agree with that argument to the extent that some circumstances are more difficult than others. But regardless of our outer circumstances, we still use our thinking to connect events and experiences to either good or evil. If you believe that evil is "out there," you will see evil; you will find it, and guess what, it will find you.

However, if you look for love, beauty, charity, you'll be able to see love, beauty, and charity in those otherwise neutral places. Our beliefs determine our feelings about our power, and much of what creates a feeling of powerlessness in us is due only to our beliefs. These feelings of powerlessness emerge out of our unconscious reactions to the world and manifest as frustration, anger, and impatience. Road rage? The traffic isn't out to get you.

27. Who Is the Most Powerful Person on the Planet?

We can get a truer control of our lives by adjusting our beliefs to reflect two realities: one, the world is neutral—neither good nor evil, not "out to get us"—and two, the one thing in the world that we can control is ourselves. That means controlling our ideas and *learning* to use our personal power to find and create love while shifting attention away from anger and fear.

If we're immediately threatened, fear is an appropriate reaction that we should pay attention to. Fear is fight-or-flight, which makes evolutionary sense if there is a real threat. If I'm an ancient tribesman hunting gazelle out on the African savannah, that fight-or-flight response can mean the difference between life and death when there are omnipresent dangers like fanged, clawed, and venomous cohabitants sharing my turf. But when we no longer live in small tribes competing with carnivores and in deadly warfare with other primate tribes, this Stone Age nervous system is a dangerous relic.

The last ten thousand years of evolution and the great teachings of the Buddha and Christ *should count for something*. Those who try to sell us fear as a "justification" for politics or deodorant are appealing to Stone Age consciousness, ignoring ten thousand years of consciousness evolution. As we have become more complicated thinkers in more complicated powerful social groups, for the most part modern man no longer faces constant, lethal dangers. If the whole human race could reimagine our ideas about fear and move to a more compassionate understanding about each other, there would be enough in the world for *everyone's* survival. There would be more than enough room for every religion and every color and sexual orientation. Yet look around. Yikes! Most of us haven't rethought our Stone-Age reactions to modern circumstances.

If we can learn to reimagine which things *really* affect us, we would no longer have to be at the mercy of our fear beliefs. This is what is called "mindfulness": keeping your attention only on things that you can control. Mindfulness is the foundation of self-knowledge—seeing what we can and cannot control. It enables you to observe the habits and beliefs that lead you away from your personal power.

We don't have to believe what our parents believe, or what our religion teaches, or what we learn in school. Mindfulness is the first step to real power. Making yourself the most powerful person in the world means noticing that your feelings, and then your reactions—for good or for evil—can properly come under your control.

The fact is, we have the power to change beliefs *now*.

To gain access to our power, we need to be willing to look at the truth and untangle the bad feelings. Yes, it will seem impossibly complicated, and it will come with a new fear of how painful it will feel. But once you unpack the pain and see how much you've created and what part is from otherwise neutral sources, you'll start to gain power over pain. If you get a bad grade on a test, how much is from not studying enough? If you get a speeding ticket, you were probably driving too damn fast; it wasn't because the officer didn't like your car. If you find yourself trying to justify your bad grade or your speeding ticket, you should be aware that self- righteousness—the need to make yourself right and others wrong—is a guarantee that you will create pain in your life.

If you would be truly powerful, consider this powerful way of thinking about love: love is like light. If you want to see by the light, you must first be the light. Your power resides in recognizing that light and energy within you. That light and energy within is connected to the one light and energy we all come from. You

27. Who Is the Most Powerful Person on the Planet?

can tap into that energy as much or as little as you want. Being mindful is seeing what you can control and controlling those things with love. If you can do that, your light will reveal to you those things you can't control, and you can let go of them. You were born with the power of that light coded into your soul. Why not receive that power with blessing and gratitude?

Sweat This Out

Go grab your notebook one last time. We'll do two simple exercises to help develop your mindfulness.

Noticing your power: Jot down a list of any and everything that bothers you, annoys you or irritates you (government regulations, dog poop on the lawn, your mother's nagging, other people's insane political views). You can include yourself in this list. Perhaps you're annoyed by your inability to lose weight, you feel stuck in your job, or you can't quit smoking.

Go down your list and check to see how much power you have with each of these things. If you do have any power, where does it begin?

For example, take your income tax. Most people think they have no power over taxation, but that's not entirely true. You have the power to pay your taxes or risk not paying them. You have the power to cheat on your taxes, and you have the power to try to elect representatives who will decide how to spend the taxes and who will levy the taxes. Mindfulness lies in seeing the power you do have and accepting what you don't.

That's real power.

AFTERWORD

If you've read the questions and honestly responded to them, my hope is that you will have shifted your gaze from "out there" to "in here," and by seeing and understanding the truth of your own heart, you feel a more inclusive and open attitude toward your relationships, your projects and vocations, your responsibilities, and possibly even your connection to all the creatures of the earth. Goodbye, fear—hello, love.

The deeper you stay focused on your own heart and mind, the deeper you will come to understand that the foremost purpose of life's energy is to love—and by loving, to serve.

I believe we're all connected to the same energy source. One of the essential dimensions to that source, which is visible in the physical world, is constant change. I think each of us has the ability to change, and when we connect to that source, we connect more consciously to our own life changes. When we resolve to examine our lives, to become more honest with ourselves, and then to communicate our truth in a clear, loving, and nonthreatening way, we will experience more joy and love, and considerably less pain and suffering.

I believe you'll find that love is contagious.

Peace in,
GWS

MY HEARTFELT PLEA TO ANYBODY THAT IS IN LOVE NOW

Are you in a relationship right now? Are you in love with the person? If you are, I want you to forget about all the issues you have with them for the moment. Go outside *this very minute* and look up to the heavens. Whether it's day or night, cold or hot, raining or snowing, sleeting or hailing, whether you believe in a God or not, whether you're sick or healthy, look up at the sky and give thanks for being one of the chosen among the seven billion-plus people on this planet who have been given the greatest gift there is and ever will be. GO OUTSIDE RIGHT NOW, look up, and say, "Thank you, Creator (or Spirit or God or whatever is out there) for allowing me the opportunity to feel the greatest feeling any human could ever feel. I am going to do everything in my power to acknowledge this feeling every day so I never forget how truly blessed I am to be in love and to have my beloved in my life. I am going to do my best every day, regardless of how difficult it seems at times, to work on loving them unconditionally. Thank you again for the gift of love."

ACKNOWLEDGMENTS

I have some wonderful people to thank for being a part of this book coming into being, and I'd like to acknowledge their help, support, and guidance.

Keith Darcy, the brilliant and beautiful ethicist who was always willing to engage with me on any and all subjects under the sun. It was one of our early morning talks that was the catalyst that got me started on this writing journey.

Margaret Harris, who strongly suggested that I chill on the five hours a day of drumming practice and use my mind to make something happen.

Sherri Dreyfuss, for being my first editor and giving me lots of positive feedback and continued support throughout the process.

Charles Stafford, for recommending I seek out Dr. Patrick McCord if I wanted to write a "real" book.

Bennett Burbank, for suggesting I cut down the number of questions.

Cory Baker, for giving me his time and his brain power and his continued belief that I actually had something worthwhile to say.

Barbara Colombo, for her incredibly enthusiastic and positive encouragement after reading one of the earliest drafts, for her big-brained editorial wisdom, and for continuing to believe in this project even when I was having trouble. So grateful for the faith, Boulda.

Mark Friedman, for giving me his undivided attention every morning for two months and sharing all of his monster editorial and brain skills with me.

Lou Gianonne, for always being there to listen to me, to share with me, to argue with me, to challenge me, and to comfort me. Thank you for being my best friend and always believing in me and rooting for me. And most importantly, for coming up with the subtitle for the book! I'm so grateful to have you in my life.

Claudia Volkman, for her awesome editorial skills and for making the interior design so clean and attractive.

Karen Strauss, for giving me the opportunity of sharing my ideas with the world.

And to my editor, compatriot, and co-pilot on this journey, *Dr. Patrick McCord.* This book would not have been possible without his willingness to argue with me and struggle with me and share his overdeveloped brain, his expanding heart, and his incredibly tender soul until the last word was punched into the computer.

I am deeply grateful to all of you for believing in me and believing in this project. And if there is anyone I have forgotten, please know that in my heart you are thanked.

www.ingramcontent.com/pod-product-compliance
Lightning Source LLC
Chambersburg PA
CBHW052053110526
44591CB00013B/2190